"These materials _____
liever in an interactive, personal discovery p_____
God's purposes for fruitful and victorious living."

Dr. John Orme, Executive Director,
Interdenominational Foreign
Mission Association

"Some of the best discipleship materials I have seen. I appreciate the centrality of Scripture and the Christ-centered focus."

Dr. Hans Finzel, Executive Director,
CBInternational

"The power of these books comes from the lifestyle of two people who practice these truths and teach them to others."

Barry St. Clair, Founder and Director,
Reach Out Ministries

"This discipleship curriculum is easy to read and easy to use. I heartily recommend it for [those] who desire to know Christ and make Him known."

Dr. George Murray, President,
Columbia International University,
former General Director of
The Evangelical Alliance Mission (TEAM)

DARING DISCIPLE SERIES

Discovering Your Identity

BILL JONES AND TERRY POWELL

Christian Publications
CAMP HILL, PENNSYLVANIA

Christian Publications, Inc.
3825 Hartzdale Drive, Camp Hill, PA 17011
www.cpi-horizon.com
www.christianpublications.com

Faithful, biblical publishing since 1883

Discovering Your Identity
ISBN: 0-87509-893-2
LOC Catalog Control Number: 00-131982
© Copyright 2000 by
Crossover Communications International.

Printed in the United States of America

00 01 02 03 04   5 4 3 2 1

For information, write:
Crossover Communications International
Box 211755
Columbia SC USA 29221

Dedication

To Lauren Elizabeth Jones

As you live out who you are in Christ,
may you be consecrated and victorious
for His glory,

and

To Dolly Powell

No aspect of my earthly identity
is more valuable to me than this:
I am "Dolly's husband."

CONTENTS

Introduction

*D*iscovering Your Identity is a Bible study guide for your individual benefit. This discipleship material will have maximum profit for you if you're a part of a group that meets on a weekly basis. A *Leader's Guide* for *Discovering Your Identity* is available from the publisher.

Other titles in the Daring Disciple Series include:

Knowing God
Walking in the Spirit
Learning to Trust
Sharing the Message

CHAPTER ONE

The Importance of Identity

Go to Bangkok and visit the Temple of the Golden Buddha. It is small, perhaps thirty square feet. But you will be impressed by the ten-and-a-half-foot solid-gold statue of Buddha. It weighs two and a half tons and has a monetary value of $196 million. Look around and you will also notice a glass case containing an eight-inch-by-twelve-inch piece of clay and an inscription describing the statue's history.

In 1957 a group of monks from a monastery relocated a clay Buddha from their temple to a new location. The monastery had to be moved to make room for a new highway through Bangkok. When the crane lifted the giant idol, a crack occurred in the clay. What's more, rain began to fall. The head monk, concerned about damage to the sacred Buddha, lowered the statue back to the ground and covered it with a large canvas tarp to protect it from the rain.

Later that evening, he checked on the Buddha by shining his flashlight under the tarp to see if the Buddha was dry. As the light reached the crack, he noticed a little gleam shining back and thought it strange. As he took a closer look at this gleam of light, he wondered if there was something underneath the layer of clay. He fetched a chisel and hammer from the monastery and began to chip away at the clay. As he knocked off a few shards, the gleam grew brighter and bigger. After hours of labor, the monk stood face-to-face with the extraordinary solid-gold Buddha.

Historians believe that several hundred years before the head monk's discovery, the Burmese army was about to invade Thailand (then called Siam). The Siamese monks, realizing that an attack was imminent, covered their precious golden Buddha with an outer covering of clay in hopes that it would keep their treasure from being looted by the Burmese. Unfortunately, the Burmese slaughtered all the Siamese monks, and the well-kept secret of the golden Buddha remained intact until that fateful day in 1957.[2]

The Golden Buddha's story is analogous to that of many contemporary Christians. They are persons of infinite value, worth far more than the gold employed in sculpting the statue. Yet they see themselves as clay—inferior, unappealing and insignificant. Their self-image is rooted in external considerations rather than what is inside. They are deceived concerning their true identity and value—all because they don't know or appropriate the truth in God's Word concerning their position in Christ.

This book's purpose is to serve as a hammer and chisel, chipping away at the misconceptions that shape the way some believers see themselves. As you look into the mirror of God's Word from week to week, your reflection may surprise you. You'll see yourself as God sees you. You may have to shade your eyes from the gleam!

In this study, you will delve into Scripture for perspective on the following questions:

- Who am I?

- How does my relationship with Jesus Christ affect my identity?

- What biblical concepts can help me discard the clay and see the truth about what I am?

- What are the cultural standards that cloud my vision of my identity?

- How can awareness of my position in Christ affect behavior and relationships?

- How does a biblical self-esteem result in a selfless, rather than a self-centered, lifestyle?

The focus of this initial chapter is to help you discern why an accurate self-portrait is integral to vibrant Christian living. What follows are characteristics of an *inappropriate* self-concept.

An improper self-concept is . . .

Influenced by culture rather than the Bible

Typically, folks in contemporary society employ false values when determining personal significance.

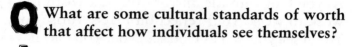

Q **What are some cultural standards of worth that affect how individuals see themselves?**

A _____

_____

_____

Your list probably includes one or more of the following criteria:

1. *Appearance.* James Dobson calls physical attractiveness "the most highly valued personal attribute in our culture."[3] Just look at the number of advertisements that promise relief from "plagues" such as baldness, wrinkled skin or gray hair. How a person looks determines how others behave toward him. From the self-consciousness of early adolescence to the alarm of middle-age bulges, many folks equate appearance with worth.

Yet a look into the mirror of Scripture contradicts the world's emphasis on physical beauty. Soak up the words of First Samuel 16:7. When inspecting Jesse's sons to determine which one God had selected to be king, even the prophet Samuel placed too much emphasis on appearance.

Q What timeless truth about human worth or identity does the verse offer?

A _____

_____

_____

_____

2. *Achievement*. Some individuals are granted worth by society if they are exceptionally gifted. Whether the area of ability is athletics, music or public speaking, their identity is rooted in competence that others observe and applaud. What they achieve is what they think gives them significance.

We aren't encouraging you to become an underachiever. Just don't allow cultural attitudes toward ability to be the foundation of your identity.

Skim the narrative in Luke 10:1-20. Jesus recruited seventy people for a short-term itinerant ministry. Upon returning, they gave glowing testimonies of ministry achievements, including the exorcism of demons. Jesus acknowledged that He had given them authority over Satan. Then, in 10:20, He put their ministry achievement in proper perspective. After inspecting 10:20, complete the following sentence.

**The source of the disciples' significance was not_____,
but_____.**

3. *Aptitude.* When it comes to perceived value, whoever has a high IQ or an area of extraordinary mental acumen has an advantage over the rest of us who are "average." The math whiz, computer expert or SAT wizard has a status level in others' eyes that most of us cannot touch even when we are standing on tiptoe.

Q Examine the following Bible verses. **How does each reference rate mental aptitude and knowledge as the primary basis for your identity?**

A (a) Proverbs 1:7 _____

_____

_____

A (b) Philippians 4:8 _____

_____

_____

4. *Accumulations.* One of the false values propagated by Western culture is "having." Satan disguises the truth and suggests that the more money and material things we accumulate, the more meaningful life will be and the greater significance we'll enjoy. An article in *Money* magazine concluded that material wealth is the number one obsession of Americans.[4] Similarly, a *Newsweek* magazine article described Americans as having reached a new plane of consciousness called "transcendental acquisition."[5]

Q Yet the primary antidote to error is truth. **What arguments does Scripture give to counter our culture's emphasis on accumulations as a basis for personal identity?** Jot down an answer for each of the following set of verses. (You'll discover that money has never yet made anyone rich.)

A (a) Proverbs 28:19 _____

_____

_____

A (b) Matthew 6:19-21 _____

_____

_____

A (c) First Timothy 6:7-11 _____

_____

_____

Q We have sketched four cultural standards of significance or personal identity: appearances, achievement, aptitude and accumulations. **Which of these false measures of worth has most often victimized you? Explain.**

A _____

_____

_____

_____

An inappropriate self-concept . . .

Originates with Satan rather than with God

The false benchmarks for identity stem from a world system or mind-set influenced by Satan himself. Paul referred to people who "walked according to the course of this world, according to the prince of the power of the air" (Ephesians 2:2). Later in the same letter he referred to Satan and his demons as "rulers . . . powers . . . spiritual forces of wickedness in the heavenly places" (6:12). The term "devil" means "slanderer" or "deceiver." His goal is to deceive you concerning your true identity and the benefits you have as a Christian.

What Satan wants you to believe about personal identity is the polar opposite of God's opinion. When you peer into the mirror of God's Word, you see the truth about who you are. You are created in God's own image (Genesis 1:26-27). Despite the marring of that image by sin, Ephesians 4:24 says to "put on the new self, which in the likeness of God has been created in righteousness and holiness of the truth." Whereas Satan's goal for your life is destructive (John 10:10; 1 Peter 5:8), God's is constructive (2 Corinthians 3:18).

Who you believe concerning your identity is the crucial variable in forming your self-image.

An improper self-image . . .

Expresses itself in different ways

An improper, shaped-by-the-world self-image invokes mental pictures of a weak, servile, doubting person. Someone who brightens up any room—by leaving it! Someone who feels inferior. Someone who lacks confidence due to an overwhelming sense of inadequacy. But low self-esteem is only one logical expression of an improper personal identity. **According to Romans 12:3, what different attitude may stem from an inaccurate self-identity?**

Ironic, isn't it? Pride as well as inferiority grows from the soil of an unbiblical view of self. Improper self-esteem may be positive, but it is still wrong. Whether the diagnosis is low self-image or an excessively high self-concept, the result is the same: *self-centeredness* that limits one's capacity to enjoy fellowship with God and serve Him effectively.

Q **When your self-concept is unhealthy, how does it show? In an attitude of inferiority or pride? Explain.**

A _____

_____

_____

_____

An unhealthy identity . . .

Relies on others' opinions, rather than God's

More often than not, what others think of us is the primary influence in shaping our self-image and sense of security. Their opinion validates that we are either somebody significant or somebody unworthy of attention. Their verbal strokes enhance our self-esteem; their disapproval damages it. Unfortunately, most people evaluate us on the basis of the false values described previously.

Yet the only stable premise for a proper self-concept is in God's opinion of us. Nobody has said anything worse about us than God: He calls us sinners (Romans 3:23) whose hearts, naturally-speaking, are "deceitful . . . desperately sick" (Jeremiah 17:9). And nobody has said anything better about us than God: He created us in His own image (Genesis 1:26-27), and He loved us enough to send His Son, Jesus, to die in our place (John 3:16). As we respond to His unconditional love, our self-identity is validated, liberating us from the need to use others to verify our sense of worthiness.

One young man in Mississippi had a father who was a dental surgeon. The dad exerted pressure on his son to follow in his footsteps and become a dentist. When the young man was turned down for dental school, his father chided him and constantly reminded him of his failure. He absorbed his father's opinion and began perceiving himself as a failure. As a result, he became an underachiever who dropped out of church and fled from fellowship with the Lord. His whole identity was shaped by his father. But by the wrong father! Relying on our heavenly Father's perspective has a positive, rather than a degrading, effect on our lives.

Q Think back over the past years of your life. **Whose opinion have you relied on most of-**

ten in order to verify your significance as a person? Explain.

A _____

_____

_____

Q What consequences have you experienced as a result of basing your identity on human opinion instead of God's?

A _____

_____

_____

An improper personal identity . . .

Invites negative rather than positive feelings

According to Proverbs 23:7, "As [a man] thinks within himself, so he is." When improper sources and values shape our thinking, the result is a barrage of adverse emotions and attitudes, such as:

- a sense of isolation and loneliness.

- a sense of constantly falling short of peoples' or God's expectations, of never quite measuring up.

- shame or a sense of unworthiness.

- a lack of confidence in relationships or at work.

- insecurity.

- a feeling that we are unworthy to be loved or cherished.

- inability to accept criticism or reproof; sensitive ego.

- deep-rooted sense of guilt even when we have confessed sin or cannot pinpoint a sin to confess.

What follows is a cycle or pattern we experience when improper sources or standards affect our identity:

Effect of Improper Input on Feelings and Behavior

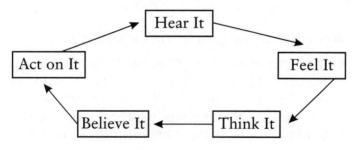

Concerning one's self-image . . .

Its influence is pervasive rather than restrictive

As suggested by the previous diagram, an improper personal identity has a sobering impact on various spheres of life: our feelings, our beliefs, our conduct and our interpersonal relationships. And here's the bottom line for us as Christians: *An improper self-image hinders our capacity to serve God and others. We're too wrapped up either in our emotional pain or arrogance to live as an others-centered disciple.* In contrast, a biblical self-esteem enables us to love others because our own identity is settled. Relying on biblical truth for a proper self-identity frees us from self-preoccupation and releases us to give without concern for others' validation of our worth. And when we view ourselves through the lens of Scripture, we are more apt to involve ourselves in ministry—since we are not so afraid of failure and since we are motivated by God's glory rather than our own. Open your Bible to Exodus 3:7-4:15.

Q **How would you describe Moses' self-image?**

A _____

_____

_____

Q **How did his negative view of himself affect his attitude toward and motivation for ministry?**

A _____

_____

_____

Q Moses' excuses revealed improper feelings, thoughts and beliefs about his identity. His focus was on himself rather than on what God wanted to do with and through him. **How did God respond to Moses' excuses?**

A _____

_____

_____

Q Moses almost missed God's will for his life because of improper attitudes toward himself. He illustrated the pervasive effect of improper self-esteem. **Have you ever hesitated or refused to participate in ministry because an unhealthy self-concept permeated your thinking? Explain.**

A _____

_____

_____

Q At the opposite end of the spectrum from Moses was the apostle Paul. **What effects did a more biblical personal identity have on him?** (See Galatians 1:15-17; 1 Timothy 1:12-17.)

A _____

_____

_____

An unhealthy self-esteem . . .

Is changeable, rather than fixed

The forces that shape an inappropriate personal identity are powerful. One's self-image takes years to formulate. Negative impressions are deeply rooted in one's psyche. Yet the image is not inalterable. The Holy Spirit, working in tan-

dem with the written Word He inspired, transforms a person's self-concept.

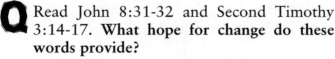 Read John 8:31-32 and Second Timothy
3:14-17. **What hope for change do these
words provide?**

A _____

_____

_____

Determining Who You Are

The remainder of this book counteracts cultural
factors shaping personal identity and zeroes in on
Bible truths about your identity in Christ. The organizational framework for the studies is Ephesians
1:3-7, though you will probe other pertinent parts
of Scripture as well. You'll discover that highfalutin
doctrinal terminology has practical implications for
the way you view yourself and the way you function
in the warp and woof of daily living. By increasing
your awareness of spiritual blessings and your position in Christ, a healthier personal identity will crys-
tallize in your thinking.

Memorizing Scripture

To set the stage for the following chapters,
memorize Romans 12:2. This first memory verse
emphasizes the contrast between the world's
value system and God's.

It is possible to have a sound theology without having a sound life. But we cannot have a sound life without having a sound theology. Theology must never be viewed as an abstract science. It is a matter of life and death.[1]

—R.C. Sproul

You Are Personally Chosen

Several years ago I (Terry) received a harsh letter from a lawyer, informing me that a woman was suing me over an auto accident that had occurred a year earlier. The suit asked for a jury trial, $30,000 in remuneration, plus punitive damages, the amount of which would be decided by the court. Since my liability insurance covered up to $25,000, there was an outside possibility of losing big bucks. I bit my fingernails to the quick at the prospect.

Though my improper turn completely demolished her Buick, the woman seemed physically fit at the scene of the accident. The insurance company representative confirmed my suspicions and said she was trying to rip me off. When my insurer refused to pay her exaggerated monetary claims, she hired a lawyer and filed the suit. That's when the insurer hired its own lawyer and a series of

phone calls and letters seeking accident information was initiated.

Over a nine-month period, I heard several horror
stories about individuals who were victims of un-
ethical lawsuits, yet who lost their court cases. One
fellow wound up losing his business and his house
over a suit that he seemingly had no chance of winning. Occasionally I would lie awake at night, worrying about the status of the lawsuit, wondering if a
jury would fall for her fraudulent injury claims.

Finally I phoned the insurance company to see
why the process was taking so long and if a court
date had been scheduled. I discovered that the suit
had been settled out of court six months earlier!
The insurance company had forgotten to inform
me of the fact. The amount she received was well
under the $25,000 liability coverage.

Imagine! A fact I was not aware of had negatively affected the quality of my life over a
six-month period. Had I known the suit was settled and I was in no danger of losing money, I
would have slept better and worried less. Musing
on that experience, I discovered the hard way that
what you don't know *can* hurt you. Keeping in-
formed definitely pays dividends.

Knowing the Scoop

That is true in the spiritual realm too. When we
are uninformed concerning biblical truths and prin-
ciples of living, what we don't know can stunt our
spiritual growth and usefulness to God. That's why

we must fight the world's pull toward an unhealthy self-image with the weapon of Scripture. Truths about our position in Christ will instill a balanced, biblical self-concept. When it comes to God's opinion of who you are, in this chapter you will discover the infinite value of knowing the scoop!

Before delving into the first truth concerning your position in Christ, digest the following overview of the book's concepts. Figure 1 reveals unhealthy feelings far too typical, even among Christians. Then it responds with biblical ideas that oppose the erroneous identities instilled by false values. Though other Bible passages will be incorporated, the chart also indicates that each key concept of the book originates in Ephesians 1:3-7.

Making the Team

After a recent NBA finals, the cover of *Sports Illustrated* depicted Michael Jordan releasing the ball. Just two words formed the caption: "THE SHOT." In a classic instance of déjà vu, Jordan's jump shot carried the Chicago Bulls over the Utah Jazz—their sixth basketball title of the 1990s!

No athlete in the world has been more recognized than Jordan. Back in the early 1980s, he hit the winning basket for North Carolina's NCAA Championship. Ten times an NBA scoring champion. Perennial member of the league's all-defensive team. League MVP. All-star game MVP. Thirty million plus annual salary, even more from TV commercials and shoe endorsements. Say the name "Michael Jordan" in a

FIGURE 1-Discovering Your Identity in Christ

YOU MAY FEEL	IN FACT YOU ARE	BECAUSE OF THE TRUTH OF	BASED ON EPHESIANS 1:3-7
Left out	Personally chosen	Election	"Chose us"
Like a failure	Officially holy	Justification	"Holy"
Ashamed, hopeless	Supernaturally transformed	Regeneration	"Blameless"
Rejected	Irrevocably accepted	Reconciliation	"Before Him"
Unloved	Totally loved	Substitution	"In love"
Insecure/Fearful	Incredibly secure	Adoption	"Adopted us"
Worthless	Obviously valuable	Redemption	"Redemption"
Guilty	Notably forgiven	Propitiation	"Forgiveness"

crowded playground in Russian-speaking Ukraine, and the kids swarm to you repeating his name—perhaps the only English words they've ever learned.

How do you think Jordan's ninth-grade basketball coach feels now? You know, the one who cut Michael from the team after tryouts. The one who concluded he wasn't good enough for the bench, much less the starting lineup. Yes, even Michael Jordan knows what it's like not to be chosen. To feel left out.

Do *you* ever feel left out spiritually speaking? Ever wonder if you belong on God's team? Ever doubt that God's plan includes you? Even bona fide Christians feel that way occasionally. Because they give too much credence to their feelings, their self-image or sense of identity suffers. It's time to identify a rock-ribbed truth: If you have put your faith in Christ at some point in the past, it's because God has personally chosen you!

Let's dissect that truth and its practical implications for you.

Identity under Construction

The fact that God chose you is a foundation stone in the construction of a healthy personal identity. Ephesians 1:3 refers to "spiritual blessing[s]" you have in Christ. The verses that follow list specific divine favors Paul had in mind. The phrases we've italicized represent the basis for this chapter:

> Blessed be the God and Father of our Lord Jesus Christ, who has blessed us with every spiritual blessing in the heavenly places in Christ, just as

He chose us in Him before the foundation of the world, that we would be holy and blameless before Him. In love *He predestined us* to adoption as sons through Jesus Christ to Himself, *according to the kind intention of His will,* to the praise of the glory of His grace, which He freely bestowed on us in the Beloved. In Him we have redemption through His blood, the forgiveness of our trespasses, according to the riches of His grace. (Ephesians 1:3-7, emphasis added)

Why did God choose you? Because He has a *plan* for you, a *purpose* for you and a *place* for you.

Knowing God's Plan

That God chose you for salvation indicates that He has a plan for you. His ultimate aim for your life is couched in Romans 8:29: "For those whom He foreknew, He also predestined *to become conformed to the image of His Son . . .*" (italics are mine). Yet His desire for Christlikeness in you is hindered by the reality of sin. So whatever His plan is for you, it must deal with the issue of sin and your relationship to it.

Scripture reveals God's threefold agenda for removing this obstacle to Christlikeness. Look up the verses that follow and try to identify each phase of His plan concerning your relationship to sin.

PHASE 1

Q Mull over Romans 6:23. **What consequence of sin did Paul cite?**

A _____

_____

_____

_____

Q Turn to Second Corinthians 5:21 and Galatians 3:13. **How did God the Father resolve the problem of sin's consequence?**

A _____

_____

_____

The biblical term "salvation" means "deliverance." It suggests that we are facing some type of danger and need to be snatched away and brought to a place of safety. The Old Testament concept of salvation often refers to Israel's physical deliverance from an enemy nation. Applied to Christian experience, the term refers to the initiative God took in delivering you from the ultimate penalty of sin—death, eternal separation from God. Because God is perfect, He cannot enter into a relationship with anyone who is imperfect. Unless that person's sin is paid for in full. That is where Jesus came in. Though He "knew no sin" (2 Corinthians 5:21), He died on the cross to make your relationship with God the Father possible. He became sin for us (see 5:21) and "redeemed us from the curse of the Law" (Galatians 3:13).

To summarize, here is **Phase 1** of God's plan: *He saved you from the penalty of sin.*

PHASE 2

Despite deliverance from the long range penalty of sin within you, there's still an inclination to sin. Here's how Paul described the pull of sin that stirred within him: "I know that nothing good dwells in me, that is, in my flesh; for the willing is present in me, but the doing of the good is not. For the good that I want, I do not do, but I practice the very evil that I do not want" (Romans 7:18-19). Yet Scripture makes it clear that divine deliverance can extend to the power of sin as well as to its penalty. Put simply, a pattern of sin is *not* inevitable for a Christian. God does not choose to save you, then leave you to flounder on your own.

 Digest Romans 8:2-6. **Jot down phrases from these verses that show God's provision over sin's control of your life.**

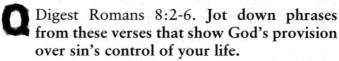

_____

_____

_____

_____

Here's **Phase 2** of the plan God has in choosing you. By sending His Spirit to reside in you, *He can deliver you from the power of sin.* His resources enable you to break free from sin as a controlling force or pattern of life.

PHASE 3

God's choice of you for salvation will ultimately result in your perfection. This final phase of His plan for you will occur at your physical death or, if you're still around, whenever Jesus returns and life as we know it ceases on planet earth.

Q Read First John 3:2-3. **What words from this text indicate that God's goal of Christlikeness will become a reality for you?**

A _____

_____

_____

Q Look again at 3:3. **How should the eventual eradication of sin's presence affect you in the here and now?**

A _____

_____

_____

Let's recap the previous pages. If you have a relationship with Christ, it is because God chose you "before the foundation of the world" (Ephesians 1:4). His choice of you stems from His plan for you. His plan for you includes:

- salvation from the *penalty* of sin
- deliverance from the *power* of sin
- ultimate rescue from the *presence* of sin.

Identifying God's Purpose

Q If God's choice of you stems from His plan for you, His plan flows from a grand purpose for your life. **What phrase in Isaiah 43:7 captures your reason for being?**

A _____

_____

_____

Imagine! You were created, then chosen by God for salvation *for His sake*! The verb *glorify* means "to cause someone or something to seem better, larger, and finer." God intends for your life to draw positive attention to Him. Paul paraphrased this concept when he said his ambition was "to be pleasing to Him" (2 Corinthians 5:9).

To discover how a Christian pleases or glorifies God, consult Mark 12:30. Complete this sentence: **More than anything else, God wants my**

_____.

Q Now list below the words in the verse describing the kind of love God desires.

A _____

_____

_____

"With all your heart" implies a single focus. Your allegiance isn't divided among competing loyalties. It refers to a deep-rooted commitment,

not primarily an emotional, euphoric state. "All
your soul" suggests a passionate, fervent love that
will often include an overflow of affection. "All
your mind" connotes a relationship fueled by
study of His Word—a rational acknowledgment
that devotion to Him is a reasonable response to
His choice of you. "All your strength" implies an
intensity about your love for Him. It doesn't vac-
illate with circumstances nor wane over time.

There is a second way to fulfill the purpose of
glorifying God. Read Matthew 28:19-20 and
complete the following sentence.

In addition to loving Him, I can glorify God by
_____.

God's purpose for you includes your participa-
tion in ministry—kingdom business! No matter
what vocation He gives you, He intends for you
to make a spiritual impact in your spheres of influence. The form of your involvement may vary:
personal witnessing, Bible teaching, financial giving—you name it! That God has significant work
reserved for you is also revealed in Ephesians
2:10: "For we are His workmanship, created in
Christ Jesus *for good works, which God prepared
beforehand so* that we would walk in them" (emphasis added).

Let's pause to glance at the rearview mirror. So
far in Chapter 2 you've discovered that *God chose
you.* He chose you because He had a plan for you:
to save you from the *penalty,* the *power* and the
presence of sin. His plan for you stems from an
overarching purpose: that you *glorify Him* (Isaiah

43:7) by living a life that *pleases Him* (2 Corinthians 5:9). Pleasing Him involves:

- *obeying the Great Commandment* (to love Him: Mark 12:30)
- *obeying the Great Commission* (to serve Him: Matthew 28:19-20)

Recognizing Your Place

God's choice of you includes a place, or places, to be more precise. Allow the following Bible passages to inform your self-concept.

According to Psalm 139:13-18, God's creation of you was intricate and rational. You were "skillfully wrought" in your mother's womb, revealing intentionality and intelligence behind your design. Then 139:17-18 provide a clincher: "How precious also are Your thoughts to me, O God! How vast is the sum of them! If I should count them, they would outnumber the sand. . . ."

To complete the following statement, find an appropriate word beginning with the letter "h." The term is conceptually related to God's thoughts concerning you.

There's a place for you in God's h___ .

Now turn to Isaiah 49:16. What God said to the chosen people of Israel is true for members of His universal church. Use material from Isaiah 49:16 to finish this sentence with another "h" word:

There's a place for you in God's h___.

Q Also read John 20:24-28, which describes one of Jesus' resurrection appearances. **How does this passage increase your appreciation for your place in the palm of God's hand?**

A _____

_____

_____

_____

To discover more about your placement with God, examine Jeremiah 31:3. Employ a different "h" word and identify yet another "place" where you reside:

There's a place for you in God's h___.

There's one more place that signifies a "spiritual blessing" God has in store for you. Enjoying it is as certain as the promise of Christ. You'll find reference to it in John 14:1-3. Find one more "h" word in your mental dictionary that fits these verses:

There's a place for you in God's h___.

The next time you feel "left out," meet those feelings head-on with the reliability of Scripture: There's a place for you in God's *head*, in God's *hands*, in God's *heart* and in God's *house*. Knowing these truths makes it difficult to sustain a low self-esteem for very long!

Why did God select you for His team? Because He has a *plan* for you involving your deliverance from sin's penalty, from sin's power and sin's presence. God's plan is prompted by a grand *purpose* for your life: to glorify Him. You bring God glory by loving Him (obeying the Great Commandment) and by serving Him (obeying the Great Commission). When you feel left out or insignificant in the eyes of God, remember: There's a place for you in His head, in His hands, in His heart and eventually in His house.

Not even Michael Jordan's assets can top those blessings!

 Which insight from this chapter means most to you right now? Why?

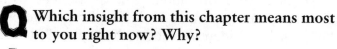

Memorizing Scripture

Tuck Romans 8:29 into the folds of your mind. This verse tells you *why* God chose you: to become conformed to the image of His Son!

If the references to predestination in this chapter have raised questions in your mind, please refer to Appendix A, "Digging Deeper."

The term "justified" . . . does not simply mean "just-as-if-I-never-sinned." That doesn't go far enough. Neither does it mean that God makes me righteous so that I never sin again. It means to be "declared righteous." Justification is God's merciful act, whereby He declares righteous the believing sinner while he is still in his sinning state.[1]

—Charles Swindoll

CHAPTER THREE

You Are Officially Holy

Here's a testimony that exposes the need for the material in this chapter:

My first full-time job came at the age of seventeen when I'd rather have been combing the beach or playing baseball. But what bothered me about that first job wasn't the work, nor was it the adventure I sacrificed for it. It was the relationship between my employer and me. As long as I arrived at least one second before 8 o'clock in the morning, took no longer than ten minutes for a break and did everything he assigned, we got along fine. But when I slipped,

33

the look on his face told me that we weren't on the best of terms. Our relationship was conditional, based on scores of "if" clauses relating directly to my performance.

That performance-based relationship describes contemporary culture. We grant acceptance or recognition to those who earn the most money, reach the highest plateau in the company, raise the best-behaved kids or exhibit the more "public" ministry gifts.

By the time I started college, I realized that to get ahead in the world, I had to achieve. With achievement would come recognition from peers as well as self-acceptance. I'd be "somebody" in the eyes of colleagues. So I taxed myself physically and mentally to achieve the highest academic average possible—a 4.0! The result? I began relating to myself on the same performance basis that I had detested on my first job, thinking accomplishment was the only proof of my value.

This performance-based identity had an adverse effect on my life in Christ. I looked at the Christian life as a pole vaulter eyes the 20-foot barrier. I worked hard and practiced my form, but deep inside I knew it was impossible.

Seeking a 4.0 average, I became defensive about any grade B or lower. When I didn't perform adequately, I became frustrated and unhappy. Failing to keep God's laws perfectly caused similar frustrations. I wanted to prove myself to God, to earn my status with Him. Since it was difficult to ac-

*cept myself apart from top performance, I pre-
sumed God accepted me on the same basis.*

   *Even after I took my first job on a large church
staff, the possibility of failure plagued my
thoughts. As long as volunteers came to my training sessions, as long as the Sunday school attendance increased, as long as the senior pastor
complimented me, I felt OK about who I was.
And only as I walked the straight and narrow line
in my Christian life did I feel accepted by God.
But when I'd blow it spiritually, days of
self-condemnation followed. I couldn't enjoy my
relationship with Christ because I kept feeling like
a poor excuse for a Christian.*

Can you identify? Does the specter of failure loom
over you and make you feel uneasy about trying new
things? Do you feel good about yourself only as long
as your performance is first-rate? Are you constantly
discouraged about the blemishes in your character,
despite obvious areas of spiritual growth since your
conversion to Christ? Do you hesitate to approach
God after you've sinned, afraid a "No Trespassing"
sign will block you from His throne?

   If so, Chapter 3 may radically change your life.
The transformation wasn't instantaneous, but meditation on the insights in this chapter freed the person whose story you read from the cramped cell of
performance orientation. Failure of any sort still
irks him. Yet he no longer gauges his personal significance on the basis of success. And he no longer
bases his acceptability before God on how he functions spiritually on any given day.

Ready to explore the Bible truth that was responsible for his jailbreak?

How in the World Can I Be Holy?

The conviction that you must meet certain standards in order to feel good about yourself is a false belief. If you have accepted Christ as your personal Savior, yet you regularly feel like you are in God's doghouse due to imperfections, that is enslavement to a lie! The consequences of these false assumptions include fear of failure, perfectionism, inability to relax, hesitancy to approach God, withdrawal from risks and the tendency to manipulate others to help you succeed. God's solution to performance orientation is a fresh awareness of your position in Christ. More specifically, *the biblical concept of justification provides raw material for construction of a sturdy identity.* Grasping this particular truth will replace erroneous criteria of worth with a trustworthy basis from Scripture.

Remember that the organizational framework for this book is Ephesians 1:3-7. Paul referred to spiritual blessings (1:3), then proceeded to list aspects of your position in Christ (1:4-7). In Chapter 2 you probed the implications of the fact that "He chose us in Him before the foundation of the world" (1:4). Now you will lock your mental lens on the phrase that follows in 1:4: "that we would be holy."

Though God wants you to live a distinctive lifestyle—to become holier over time in your attitudes and conduct—the focal point of this chapter is *not* His current behavioral expectations for you. Instead, you will concentrate on a liberating, mind-blowing fact concerning your spiritual position: *If you're a member of God's family, He already views you as holy.*

Is Self-Justification Possible?

In layman's terms, to be justified before God means to be right in His eyes, to be free from blame or guiltless before Him. It means to have legal grounds for a relationship with God. But there's a problem with human beings that makes the possibility of justification before God seem like a pipedream.

Q Read Jeremiah 17:9-10 and Romans 3:23. What factor apparently makes justification unattainable?

A _____

_____

_____

The story at the start of this chapter illustrates how performance orientation surfaces in our relationship with God. We get the idea that our status before Him depends on our efficiency at living. We may even engage in various ministries as a subtle way to earn a better standing with Him. But according to the apostle Paul, there's more bad news.

Q Read Romans 3:28 and Ephesians 2:8-9. What phrases from these verses reveal the inadequacy of performance or human effort to justify ourselves before God?

A _____

_____

_____

Being right with God comes "apart from works of the Law" (Romans 3:28). Justification is "not as a result of works, so that no one may boast" (Ephesians 2:9). If we are naturally sinful and nothing we do—no matter how grand—can make us blameless in God's sight, then we are left in a helpless state. Only outside help can resolve the dilemma. Incredibly, the God from whom we are separated intervenes.

How Does God Justify?

Q Absorb the words of Hebrews 10:10, 14; Romans 3:24; and Romans 5:1-2. What words/phrases from these verses reveal the means God used to justify sinners?

A _____

_____

_____

You learned in Chapter 2 that Jesus Christ paid the death penalty for your sin (Romans 6:23; 2 Corinthians 5:21). And, as the verses you just consulted suggest, *His* work on the cross is the means God the Father used to make you guiltless before Him. Paul said that justification comes "through the redemption which is in Christ Jesus" (Romans 3:24). Your basis for peace with God is Jesus' performance on the cross (implied in 5:1-2). You have been sanctified—declared officially holy—"through the offering of the body of Jesus Christ" (Hebrews 10:10). When you acknowledge sin and initially put your faith in Christ, God began viewing you as *perfect* (10:14), not because you are experientially flawless, but because Jesus *was* perfect and blameless, and His righteousness, positionally speaking, has been credited to your account.

At this point, a more technical definition of justification is in order.

> Justification may be defined as that act by which unjust sinners are made right in the sight of a just and holy God. The supreme need of unjust persons is righteousness. It is this lack of righteousness that is supplied by Christ on behalf of the believing sinner. Justification by faith alone means justification by the righteousness or merit of Christ alone, not by our goodness or good deeds.

> The issue of justification focuses on the question of merit and grace. Justification by faith means that the works we do are not good enough to merit justification. As Paul puts it, "By the deeds of the law no flesh will be justified in His sight" (Romans 3:20). Justification is forensic.

That is, we are declared, counted, or reckoned to be righteous when God imputes the righteousness of Christ to our account. The necessary condition for this is faith.[2]

Stuart Briscoe offers an analogy to enhance your comprehension of this awe-inspiring truth:

> I never really understood imputed righteousness until I went to work in a bank, and I was put to work on some big old ledgers. I began to understand that if you put an entry on one side of the page, you had to put an entry on the other side of the page to make everything balance. This helped me to understand that God kept books up in heaven. He had big ledgers at that time, (now he's gone on to computers but in those days He had ledgers) and I began to imagine one day that God opened His big ledger at my account. And there I saw it in divine copperplate writing: David Stuart Briscoe, and I had a little peep over His shoulder at my account and wished I hadn't, for I found against my name an awful record of sin and debt and shortcomings and failure. I was watching Him adding it all up. He came to a grand total, and I thought, "Wow! I don't like what I'm seeing." And do you know what He did next? I saw God writing against the total of my sin, in my account, these words: "Transferred to the account of the Lord Jesus Christ." I thought, "Oh, great! Fantastic!" But I remembered, "Hey, just a minute. There's got to be a double entry and I want to make sure He does it." Sure enough He did. He took down another ledger and opened it at the name of Lord Jesus Christ and

He wrote against His account the sum total of the sin of David Stuart Briscoe. And I got so excited because I looked quick back in my account and you know what I discovered there? *Nothing there!* As clean as the driven snow. And there against His name was all my sin.

Do you know, I thought that was justification. But He said, "Hold it. I haven't finished yet." Then He took the sum total of the righteousness of Jesus Christ, added it up, and wrote against it these words: "Transferred to the account of David Stuart Briscoe." Then He took the last step. He turned back to my account and under my name, would you believe it, on that clean white page, He wrote in the most magnificent writing that cannot be rubbed out, "Transferred from the account of the Lord Jesus Christ. The sum total of the righteousness of Christ credited to David Stuart Briscoe." Now, try to be miserable.[3]

Q What words in your vocabulary most accurately describe how the fact of justification makes you feel?

A _____

_____

_____

_____

Then Does Behavior Matter?

Perhaps you are thinking, "If God declared me *officially holy* when I put my faith in Christ, why

should I strive for purity in my day-to-day exis-
tence?" That is a logical question to pose. But
hammer this point deep into your consciousness:
experiential holiness still matters! Choosing to sin
does not affect a Christian's standing before God:
your spiritual position is based on Christ's holiness. Yet here are compelling reasons to stay on
the front line in your daily battle against sin:

1. *Whether you obey Christ reveals the extent of
   your love for Him.* Your deeds cannot earn His
   love. Instead, you strive to please Him because
   of His deeds on your behalf. As John put it,
   "Let us not love with word or with tongue, but
   in deed . . ." (1 John 3:18, emphasis added).
2. *God disciplines His children for disobedience.*
   His love is not weak or sentimental. He is willing to hurt His children temporarily for their
   greater long-term good. "If you are without
   discipline . . . then you are illegitimate children
   and not sons. . . . He disciplines us for our
   good, so that we may share His holiness" (Hebrews 12:8, 10). Your justification incorpo-
   rates the reality of His forgiveness. Yet His
   forgiveness does not annul sin's consequences.
   He forgave King David's adultery with
   Bathsheba. But she was still pregnant, and the
   infant died as a consequence!
3. *Sin in the life of a Christian hinders fellowship
   with God and siphons off joy.* Your secure eternal standing before God does not nullify the
   internal fallout or friction caused by sin. Scrip-

ture tells us to "exult in God" (Romans 5:11).
But that's impossible when there is a hindrance
to intimacy such as unconfessed sin.

4. *The consequences of a Christian's sin adversely
   affect other people.* Your disobedience may
   hurt those you love or even ruin your relationship with them. For instance, a man who
   deserts his wife and kids for another woman
   may eventually repent and make things right
   with God. Yet the damage to family members is
   not erased by his repentance.

So What?

How will deliberation on the doctrine of justification affect you? At first, the primary outcome occurs inside you. Gratitude to God replaces joyless
striving. Love replaces appeasement as a motive for
serving Him. You don't check your spiritual pulse
every few minutes worrying about how God per-
ceives you. A more secure personal identity
emerges. Self-condemnation occurs less frequently
because you realize that your acceptability before
God relies on what Christ has done—not on what
you do.

Billy Graham employs a courtroom scene to describe the implications of justification:

> Picture a courtroom. God the Judge is seated in
> the judge's seat, robed in splendor. You are ar-
> raigned before Him. He looks at you in terms of
> His own righteous nature as it is expressed in the
> moral law. He speaks to you:

God: John (or Mary), have you loved Me with all your heart?

John/Mary: No, Your Honor.

God: Have you loved others as you have loved yourself?

John/Mary: No, Your Honor.

God: Do you believe you are a sinner and that Jesus Christ died for your sins?

John/Mary: Yes, Your Honor.

God: Then your penalty has been paid by Jesus Christ on the cross and you are pardoned. . . . Because Christ is righteous, and you believe in Christ, I now declare you legally righteous. . . .

Can you imagine what a newspaperman would do with this event?

SINNER PARDONED— GOES TO LIVE WITH JUDGE

It was a tense scene when John and Mary stood before the Judge and had the list of charges against them read. However, the Judge transferred all of the guilt to Jesus Christ, who died on a cross for John and Mary.

After John and Mary were pardoned the Judge invited them to come to live with Him forever.

The reporter on a story like that would never be able to understand the irony of such a scene, unless he had been introduced to the Judge beforehand and knew His character.

Pardon and Christ's righteousness come to us only when we totally trust ourselves to Jesus as our Lord and Savior. When we do this, God welcomes us into His intimate favor. Clothed in Christ's righteousness we can now enjoy God's fellowship.[4]

Q How has the truth of justification affected the notions you have about God? What do you want to say to Him in response to what you've learned? Write out a prayer in the space below:

A _____

_____

_____

_____

_____

_____

_____

_____

_____

Memorizing Scripture

Memorizing Romans 5:1 will solidify the teaching of this chapter in your mind, and provide ammunition in your warfare with performance orientation.

The truth of regeneration can dispel the specter of the past. Our sins have been forgiven, and we now have tremendous capabilities for growth and change because we are new people with the Spirit of God living in us. Yes, in sinning, we will experience the destructiveness of sin and the discipline of the Father, but sin does not change the truth of who we are in Christ.[1]

—Robert McGee

CHAPTER FOUR

You Are Supernaturally Transformed

Defiant. Cold-hearted. Foul-mouthed. Those were only a few of the terms that described him as a young man. Closed-minded to a relationship with Jesus Christ, he worked on a ship that transported slaves between Africa and England. That was before he became a pastor and fought tooth and nail to end the slave trade. That was before he wrote the most beloved hymn of all time: "Amazing Grace." That was before he was supernaturally transformed. Meet John Newton.

*　　*　　*

He never finished the equivalent of elementary school. Every Christian who met him came away with a sobering realization of his spiritual darkness. Biblically illiterate, he started attending church as a young man to please his uncle, for whom he worked in a shoe store. His Sunday school teacher, burdened by the young man's spiritual insensitivity, visited the shoe store and shared the gospel of Jesus Christ with him. That was prior to his inner city ministry to kids in Chicago. That was before thousands came to Christ as a result of his preaching. That preceded his establishment of a Bible institute that now bears his name. That was before he was dramatically changed. Meet Dwight L. Moody.

*   *   *

He was religious to a fault, but totally opposed to the teachings of Christianity. He thought it preposterous that Jesus was the Messiah. His pedigree and achievements were the objects of his trust, his route to heaven. To show his contempt for proponents of faith in Christ, he aggressively pursued their arrest and imprisonment. That's what he was like before a risen Christ intervened. That described him before he hitchhiked across the ancient world, proclaiming Jesus Christ as the only means of salvation. That was before he wrote letters of instruction and encouragement that now comprise a large chunk of the New Testament. That was prior to a 180-degree turnaround. Meet the apostle Paul.

✳   ✳   ✳

Humanly speaking, the spiritual state of these three historical figures appeared hopeless. The possibility of a noticeable metamorphosis seemed remote. Then something happened inside them. Something that opened a mind closed to God's truth. Something that ignited a spark and thawed a heart frozen rock-solid by disobedience. Something that injected life into a spirit already marked for burial. Something only one Person can accomplish: the Holy Spirit. Something called *regeneration*. Because of the truth of regeneration, their autobiographies could read, "Excuse me—while I change!"

Chances are you won't write a hymn that is sung in almost every known language. Or have a college named after you. Or write inspiring letters that will make the best-seller list 2,000 years after you pen them. Yet the fact of regeneration is just as pertinent to you as it was to Newton, Moody and Paul. If you know the Lord, it is a past experience with ongoing implications for the way you feel about yourself and the way you behave. Digest this chapter and you'll extract all the potential benefits from this portion of your spiritual position.

Failure to understand this facet of your identity in Christ results in subpar living caused by a flawed self-image. Even if you've experienced regeneration—and every Christian has—ignorance of its implications may leave you chained to one of the following attitudes:

- a sense of shame or embarrassment concerning who you are
- lack of self-respect or tendency for self-reproach
- feeling of hopelessness when it comes to overcoming bad habits or altering patterns of conduct
- pessimism regarding your capacity to accomplish something meaningful for Christ
- deep sense of inferiority based on past failure or as a result of comparing yourself unfavorably to others

Let's delve into this doctrine and see why it is God's solution to the false beliefs that spawn such a negative personal identity.

Solidifying Your Position

A glance in the rearview mirror shows the route you've traveled so far in this book. You discovered that false values or cultural standards often determine a person's self-image. Instead, your identity should be rooted in facts about your position in Christ which Paul called "spiritual blessing[s]" (Ephesians 1:3).

You were personally chosen by God (1:4). He chose you because He has a plan for you: to save you from the penalty, the power and ultimately the presence of sin. His plan stems from His overarching purpose for your life: to glorify God by loving and serving Him. Fulfilling that purpose is possible because there is a special place for you in God's head, His hands, His heart and eventually His house.

Since He personally chose you for salvation, *you are officially holy* (1:4). Thanks to Christ's death on the cross, your sins are forgiven, plus all the righteousness of Christ has been credited to your moral bank account. Knowing that your acceptability to God the Father depends on Christ's work and not your own frees you from fear of failure and a performance-based personal identity.

We also derive the theme of this chapter, at least indirectly, from the wording in Ephesians 1:4. You are *"blameless before Him"* (emphasis added). This blameless state—rooted in justification and your position as "officially holy"—was made possible by an act of God known as "regeneration." Though regeneration and justification are not mutually exclusive concepts, regeneration merits its own investigation and adds a crucial building block to the construction of your identity in Christ. The next few pages reveal the practical implications of what God did for you through regeneration. You will encounter truths that combat shame, hopelessness and self-accusation.

Understanding Regeneration

Titus 3:5 is chock-full of terms that describe what happened at conversion: "He saved us, not on the basis of deeds which we have done in righteousness, but according to His mercy, *by the*

washing of regeneration and renewing by the
Holy Spirit" (emphasis added). The word *regener-*
ation stems from two Greek terms that mean "to
birth again" or "born again."

As far as God is concerned, your spiritual rebirth (regeneration) resulted in justification, thus
launching a process that obliterated all sin from
your record and eliminating shame. The reality of
regeneration—working in tandem with justification (Chapter 3)—means you are holy and blameless in God's sight, thus eliminating the validity of
any self-accusation over former sins.

Your rebirth also means you were supernaturally
transformed in the very core of your being. God's
Spirit thawed your cold heart and opened a closed
mind. As a result, you responded with a resounding
"Yes!" to Christ's invitation for salvation. The
Spirit's work of regeneration made you a "saint" in
God's eyes, "set apart" for an eternal relationship
with God. The fact that He radically changed you
on the inside paves the way for a progressive work
of experiential holiness. The Spirit's inward work
gives you a new basis for external change, thus erasing a sense of hopelessness.

To enhance your understanding of regeneration and its results, set your scope on Ephesians
2:1-10. According to one author's take on the
theme of this chapter, unregenerate persons have
"no disposition, inclination, or desire for the
things of God."[2]

Q In the space below, record words/phrases from Ephesians 2:1-5 which support that assertion:

A _____

_____

_____

In contrast, as a result of regeneration a person is "now disposed and inclined toward God."[3]

Q Jot down words/phrases from Ephesians 2:5-10 which bolster that claim:

A _____

_____

_____

Another element in a formal definition of regeneration says that it "occurs by God's divine initiative" and isn't owing to any effort on our part.[4]

Q What words/phrases from Ephesians 2:4-10 reflect this fact?

A _____

_____

_____

Q According to Ephesians 2:10, what is a logical outcome of the inward work of God that began with regeneration?

A _____

_____

Illustrating Regeneration

Read the narrative in Luke 19:1-9 slowly. It offers a dramatic before/after contrast owing to regeneration, as explained in Second Corinthians 5:17: "If anyone is in Christ, he is a new creature; the old things passed away; behold, new things have come."

Q What words from the text describe Zaccheus before he met Christ?

A _____

_____

Most tax-gatherers pocketed more money than necessary in fulfilling their duties for the Roman empire. The fact that "he was rich" (Luke 19:2) suggests he padded his own bank account by cheating others. His unscrupulous ways are also implied in 19:7. Residents of Jericho labeled Zaccheus a sinner, grumbling over Jesus' visit to his house.

Q What action on Zaccheus' part indicates that God's Spirit had sparked an interest in Jesus Christ?

A _____

_____

Q What evidence do you see in these verses that a transformation occurred *inside* him?

A _____

_____

How did the supernatural transformation (rebirth) within Zaccheus express itself out-wardly?

A _____

_____

_____

What a portrait of regeneration! An unsavory tax collector with no disposition toward Christ was radically changed on the inside, resulting in an *open mind* concerning the report he had heard about Jesus (19:3-4). Then he *opened his house* (19:5-6) and *opened his heart* (implied, vs. 9) to Christ. The inward work of God's Spirit resulted in an *open wallet* (19:8). Financial restitution was Zaccheus' outward expression of an inward reality. He knew the same power that changed him on the inside could be trusted to facilitate external transformation. Change occurred from the inside out, as shown in the following diagram:

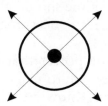

The next part of this chapter discusses your role in expressing behaviorally the internal work of re-generation. How can you cooperate with the Holy Spirit as He effects your personal transformation from the inside out? How can the real you—the "saint" that God sees within—express itself outwardly?

Applying Regeneration

As the chapter title points out, regeneration means you are supernaturally transformed! Did you notice that the title is in the *present* verb tense?

It's true that your regeneration was a past occurrence. What the Holy Spirit did within you led to faith in Christ, resulting in justification, or a "blameless" state before God (Ephesians 1:4). This benefit, made possible by God's work of regeneration, should have the current effect of erasing shame over who you were prior to conversion. How you perceive yourself in the present should be positively shaped by past realities.

However, the removal of shame is not the only practical outcome of regeneration. The fact that you became a "new creature" (2 Corinthians 5:17) at a point in time should also eradicate feelings of hopelessness concerning ongoing behavioral change.

The same divine power that lit a fire in your cold heart enables you to make transformation a continual process. Knowing what He once did should instill faith in what He can continue to do. Relying on the One who originally transformed you results in optimism in your battle with bad habits or negative behavior patterns. It is this ongoing confidence in God's power that Paul had in mind in Second Corinthians 3:18. He said that he and his readers *"are* being transformed" (emphasis added) into the image of the glory of the Lord. Zaccheus' spiritual awakening (God's initiative) resulted in a different belief system inside him. He believed that behavioral change was now possible, resulting in choices (Zaccheus' initiative) that revolutionized his business practices.

Your responsibility in the ongoing transformation process is to appropriate the benefits of regeneration. To appropriate means "to take for one's own use" or "to claim the benefits inherent in a gift or opportunity provided by someone else." That involves choosing conduct that pleases the Lord, resisting temptation and seeking Him through regular times of prayer and Bible study. As you choose to use the resources for spiritual growth at your disposal, your "position" of blamelessness before the Lord becomes an experiential reality.

Your appropriation responsibility is implied by a series of instructions in Paul's letters. He described the role that your will plays in order to experience a continued transformation into Christlikeness. Base your answers to the following questions on Ephesians 4:17-32 and Colossians 3:1-17.

Q What characterized your "old self" prior to your conversion to Christ?

What characterizes the "new self" as a result
of coming to Christ?

 _____

_____

_____

Positionally, the distance between your "old self"
and your "new self" is greater than the circumfer-
ence of the globe. Experientially, you are in process.
You still grapple with aspects of your former lifestyle. Incorporating the marks of newness into your
character is often a three-steps-forward, two-steps-
back routine. Yet Paul's lifestyle commands imply
that we have no excuses for disobedience. *The Lord
enables you for what He expects of you.* The supernatural power that invaded you at regeneration is
still within you. "It is God who is at work in you,
both to will and to work for His good pleasure"
(Philippians 2:13).

Glance again at your notes on Ephesians
4:17-32 and Colossians 3:1-17.

 Which aspect of the "old self" still characterizes you to some extent?

 _____

_____

_____

 Which mark of the "new self" is most foreign
to your current experience?

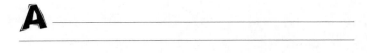

Q Review what you've learned in this "Applying Regeneration" section of the chapter. **Why can you feel confident about the possibility of transformation in these areas of struggle?**

A

Memorizing Scripture

Hiding God's Word in your heart is one thing you can do to appropriate the truth of this chapter. Committing Second Corinthians 5:17 to memory will help you experience on the outside the regenerating power you have already encountered on the inside.

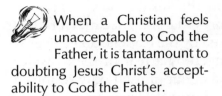
When a Christian feels unacceptable to God the Father, it is tantamount to doubting Jesus Christ's acceptability to God the Father.

CHAPTER
FIVE

You Are Irrevocably Accepted

Bob swept Carrie off her feet. After months of serious dating, she was convinced they'd get married and spend a lifetime together. Then out of the blue, he dumped her, explaining that he wanted to "sow his wild oats." Devastated, she walked around like a zombie for days, weeping a lot when she was alone. "I placed all my security on this one person," she explained. "I kept wondering what was wrong with me. Why had he rejected me? What was there about me that made me unacceptable in his eyes?" She's afraid to start dating again, figuring the same thing could happen.

*　　*　　*

Randy finds it hard to say "no," especially when someone at church asks for his time and talents. He volunteers in two separate teaching agencies and attends committee meetings several times a month. On the surface, he appears to be a self-sacrificing man who puts feet to his belief in the gospel. But on the inside, he's frantic and driven. Randy figures that if he declines a request he won't be accepted by the leaders. So he overextends himself, dogged by a fear of their displeasure. He feels good about himself only so long as he's sure of their approval. Their impression of him serves as the impetus for his decisions.

*   *   *

Feelings of isolation and loneliness haunt Steve. He's around a lot of people at church and at work. But superficiality marks even his closest relationships. He worries that if he discloses his innermost thoughts and feelings, others will keep him at arm's length. When the sharing time in his Bible study groups gets personal, he clams up. He can't risk transparency, figuring others will perceive him as unspiritual and spurn him.

*   *   *

Pam's usual prayer time is right before turning in each evening. When her spiritual performance is top-notch during the day—she takes advantage of an opportunity to witness, resists a temptation to gossip and treats her family members benevolently—she's eager to approach the Lord. Yet if she slips spiritually and fails the Lord in some way, she's hesitant to enter His presence that evening. On several occasions, doubting her acceptability before

God has even resulted in avoiding Him altogether and going straight to bed.

$$* \quad * \quad *$$

What do Carrie, Randy, Steve and Pam have in common? A fear of rejection, skepticism about their acceptability as a person. If you identify to any extent with their stories, Chapter 5 will stabilize your personal identity by acquainting you with a transforming truth: *As a Christian, you're already irrevocably accepted by the Person who matters most: God.*

Fighting Feelings with Facts

Buying into false standards of personal significance spawns poor self-esteem and hinders spiritual growth. The purpose of this book is to reorient your thinking so you base your identity on God's Word rather than worldly values. Awareness of "spiritual blessings" that constitute your position in Christ infuses you with truth that transforms attitudes as well as behavior.

During your pilgrimage on planet earth, you may occasionally feel left out or excluded. The fact is, you are *personally chosen* by God for a never-ending relationship with Him. You may see yourself as a failure, especially when it comes to following the Lord, yet because Christ's merit was credited to your account, you are *officially holy* before God. Perhaps you're ashamed of who you are or feel hopeless concerning the possibility of improving your life. But the divine power that *supernaturally transformed* you at a point in time facilitates ongoing growth in godliness.

Now the spotlight shifts to the fourth element in your spiritual position, as revealed in Ephesians 1:3-7. You are holy and blameless "before Him" (1:4). That phrase denotes a relationship with God and suggests that you're *irrevocably accepted* by Him. You aren't trespassing when you stand in His presence. You owe the privileged placement in the presence of God to the truth of *reconciliation.*

Comprehending Reconciliation

 Reconciliation is God's solution to a problem. **Turn to Isaiah 59:2 and describe the nature of that problem.**

A _____

_____

_____

Alienation from God is implied by the phrase "your iniquities have *made a separation* between you and your God" (59:2, emphasis added). His rejection of mankind is seen in the words "your sins have hidden His face from you" (59:2). Paul described the same state of estrangement between God and man. "You were formerly alienated and hostile in mind" (Colossians 1:21). "We were enemies," he insisted (Romans 5:10). Then God took the initiative to restore the broken relationship with the apex of His creation.

Q Consult Romans 5:10, Ephesians 2:13 and Colossians 1:20-22. Write words from these verses revealing the means God used to remove the enmity.

A _____

_____

_____

Reconciliation occurred "through the death of His Son" (Romans 5:10). What bridged the distance between you and God? You were "brought near by the blood of Christ" (Ephesians 2:13). Your status with God went from hostility to peace "through the blood of His cross" (Colossians 1:20). The cross is "where God gave His best for the worst in us."[1]

Previously, you examined your position in Christ in terms of *justification* (Chapter 3). Justification is a judicial term, incorporating both God's forgiveness of your sin and His imputation of Christ's righteousness to you. That's why you are free of His condemnation and the penalty of sin. It refers to the legal standing you have with God as a result of Christ's death for your sin.

Reconciliation looks at your salvation from a slightly different angle. This word captures the relational aspect of your spiritual position. It's a more personal term, suggesting fresh intimacy and union in a relationship formerly marked by antagonism. Of course, reconciliation depends on

justification. You can stand "before Him" because
He sees you as "holy and blameless."

 **How does the fact of reconciliation make
you feel?**

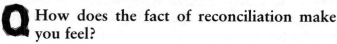

Reconciliation means that God accepts you on
the basis of Christ's performance. *His approval of
you is not in doubt because God's approval of His
Son is not in doubt*! That's the bottom-line consequence of putting faith in Christ. Here's the spin
one author put on it:

> Recently, in a group prayer meeting, some-
> one prayed, "Thank you, God, for accepting
> me when I am so unacceptable." That person
> understood that we cannot become acceptable
> through our own merit, but he seems to have
> forgotten that we are unconditionally accepted
> in Christ. *We are no longer unacceptable.* That
> is the point of the cross. Through Christ's death
> and resurrection, we have become acceptable
> to God. . . . Christ forgave our sins so that He
> could present us to the Father, holy and blame-
> less.[2]

Applying Reconciliation

Appropriating the benefits of your identity in
Christ is a process, not an instantaneous, moment-
in-time occurrence. Meditating on truths such as
reconciliation minimizes your dependence on the

world's value system and shortens the span of time in which you're governed by false beliefs about your worth. The truth of reconciliation carries practical implications for your relationships with other people as well as with God.

Q When another person rejects you—a friend, member of the opposite sex, a son or daughter, a spouse or an employer—how do you normally respond? (Be honest. Cite inward as well as behavioral reactions.)

A _____

_____

_____

Q If you're a Christian, you've learned that a perfect God accepts you and approves of you. How should that fact affect the way you respond to human rejection?

A _____

_____

Q Read Galatians 1:10. What effect did his awareness of God's acceptance have on Paul?

A _____

_____

When another person rejects you, put the painful incident in proper perspective. Tell yourself the truth. Replace what psychologists call "negative self-talk" with biblical insight. Keep fighting feelings of isolation or rejection with these words: *This person's rejection of me does not mean I am wholly unacceptable as a person. Every human being experiences rejection at some point in time. Even more important than this person's perception of me is God's perception of me. And as a Christian, He irrevocably accepts me! No matter how I feel, the fact is I have been reconciled to Him by Christ's death on the cross. He will never reject me!*

 According to Romans 5:11, what is another logical outcome of reconciliation?

 _____

_____

_____

"Exult[ing] in God" implies the capacity to *enjoy* God. You spend time with God because your heart overflows with appreciation and love. Your quiet time is prompted by genuine desire, not by a sense of stoic duty. You pray, read the Bible and involve yourself in a church because faith fills your heart as well as your head. You realize that your acceptability to Him doesn't depend on your religious duties or spiritual disciplines but on Christ's death on the cross. Because you don't fear rejection, you fall deeper and deeper in love with Him.

For yet another practical outcome of reconciliation, ponder the words of Hebrews 4:14-16 and 10:19-22. Note the following phrases:

- "Therefore let us *draw near with confidence to the throne of grace*." (Hebrews 4:16, emphasis added)
- "We have *confidence to enter the holy place*." (10:19, emphasis added)
- "Let us *draw near* with a sincere heart in full assurance of faith." (10:22, emphasis added)

 Glance back at the introduction to this chapter. Reread the account of Pam, who hesitated to pray after a spiritually subpar day. How should the truth of this lesson—and the previous Hebrews references in particular—affect her prayer life?

A _____

_____

A person who feels that his right to approach God hinges on recent performance doesn't grasp the truth of reconciliation. When Pam feels good about praying because she behaved that day, then she prays "in Pam's name" rather than "in Jesus' name." She's basing her right to meet with God on *her* work rather than Christ's. Pam needs to realize that nothing she does or fails to do on a given day affects God's acceptance of her. Nothing she does can improve upon Christ's perfection and death—and that's what gives her the right or privilege to stand before God. Perhaps she needs to confess sin. Perhaps her heavenly Father will discipline her for sin. But she's still free to approach Him.

 Now turn your attention to one more implication of reconciliation as indicated by Second Corinthians 5:18-20. What is a reasonable consequence of enjoying an intimate relationship with God?

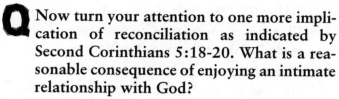

What a privilege! Because He reconciled you, you can serve as the catalyst for others' experience of reconciliation. What you've experienced, you can share. After all, one common fear of personal evangelism is no longer a hindrance—*you don't have to fear the rejection of an unbeliever, because you're irrevocably accepted by God.* (Chapter 12 offers a one-verse method for sharing your faith with non-Christians. You may want to consult that chapter now in view of the outreach response logically linked to the truth of reconciliation.)

Memorizing Scripture

To rivet the truth of Chapter 5 deeper into your consciousness, memorize Colossians 1:21-22.

You Are Totally Loved

Judy's dad pushed down hard on the career accelerator. As a ten-year-old, she was often in bed before he arrived home from work. Even on weekends he seldom held her in his lap or spent recreational time with her. How she yearned for his undivided attention, his interest in what was happening at school, his kiss upon her cheek. One year she feigned illness several times while at school. Since the family had only one car at the time, she knew her dad would have to pick her up and drive her home. Judy figured that was the only way to spend any time with her dad.

*　　*　　*

While attending a Christian college, Brad read *The Blessing* by John Trent and Gary Smalley. The book applies elements of the Jewish blessing of children in the Old Testament to contemporary family relationships. It's a call for parental expression of unconditional love through avenues such as spoken words and physical touch. Reading the book created an ache within Brad. He couldn't remember the last time either parent gave him a hug or voiced their affection. Before returning to campus after a holiday break, Brad left the book on a coffee table in his house, propped open to a dog-eared page he had marked. He told a friend back at school, "I hope they'll read it and start loving me."

Judy and Brad sought to fulfill the universal human need for love. Whether the context is the parent-child relationship, marriage or friendships, the yearning for love simmers within everyone. When our search for love is unsuccessful, the consequences are overwhelming. What is it like to feel unloved?

- There's a hole inside, an intense ache that never goes away.

- Loneliness—even in a crowd.

- A sense of desperation that often leads to depression.

- A susceptibility to unhealthy attachments with people in an attempt to feel accepted; conformity to a group.

- A tendency to fall for someone of the opposite sex before you actually know the person. You're an easy target for people who want to take advantage of you.

- Escapism—reliance on vicarious relationships through fantasies, soap operas or romance novels.

God designed human relationships as a context for meeting your innermost needs. Feeling pain over another person's rejection or lack of concern is a normal reaction, not an indication of subpar spirituality. Yet your capacity to cope with hurtful human relationships depends on the basis for your personal identity. Is your self-concept rooted in your relationship with God or with other folks in your sphere of influence? Whose love is the greater indication of your value: God's or that of other human beings? Even when you feel unloved by people who matter most to you, you can regain emotional equilibrium by remembering this fact. *You are totally loved by God!* When you're convinced of this truth, fallible human love won't devastate you or leave you vulnerable to inappropriate behavior.

So far in this book you've identified four aspects of your position in Christ:

- *You are personally chosen.*
- *You are officially holy.*
- *You are supernaturally transformed.*
- *You are irrevocably accepted.*

Add *"totally loved"* to this list of spiritual blessings. According to the final words of Ephesians 1:4, the previously discussed benefits were distributed to you "in love." What prompted God to choose you, to justify you, to transform you and to reconcile you is His love for you. Let's examine the nature of this love and the primary way in which He demonstrated it.

How Is God's Love Described?

A peek at Romans 5:6-8 reveals the extent of God's love. Here Paul paints an unflattering portrait of man, the object of divine love.

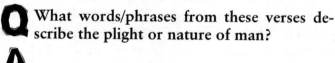

Q **What words/phrases from these verses describe the plight or nature of man?**

A _____

To love someone who is attractive or deserving is one thing. To love someone who is repulsive is another thing altogether.

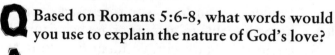

Q **Based on Romans 5:6-8, what words would you use to explain the nature of God's love?**

A _____

Don't miss Paul's point. What he said about God's love for you is light years removed from the most altruistic forms of human love. His love for you is unlimited. Unconditional. Undeserved. Nothing evil you say or do causes Him to love you less. Nothing good you say or do causes Him to love you more. Here's a prayer one young man wrote when the fact of God's love began filtering into his heart and mind:

*God, I'm glad You don't love me **because** . . .*
- *because I'm easy to love. (I'm not.)*
- *because I never take You for granted. (I do.)*
- *because I accomplish a lot for You. (I don't.)*
- *because I leave room for You in my schedule. (That's the problem: It's my schedule.)*
- *because I'm spiritually attractive. (I'm scarred from head to toe with sin.)*

*God, I'm glad You don't love me **as long as** . . .*
- *as long as I talk to You every day. (I usually find other ways to use the estimated 25,000 words the average person speaks each day.)*
- *as long as I read the letters You wrote me. (I'm too busy to write my own!)*
- *as long as I obey every commandment. (A part of me delights in skirting rules.)*
- *as long as I meet others' needs. (Preoccupation with my own needs eclipses my view of others.)*

*God, I'm glad You love me **in spite of** . . .*
In spite of myself!

Imagine! God's love doesn't hinge on your potential. It isn't prompted by your personality. It isn't a wage that depends on your performance. God's love for you is, well . . . it just *is*!

Q What effect should God's unconditional love for you have on your relationships with other people? Why?

A _____

_____

_____

Q How should His love affect the way you see and feel about yourself? Explain.

A _____

_____

_____

How Is God's Love Demonstrated?

Q Review Romans 5:6-8. All three verses refer to the main way in which God demonstrated His love for you. **What expression did His love take?**

A _____

_____

_____

Three times Paul referred to Jesus' death as the ultimate evidence of God the Father's love. Put simply, Jesus was our *substitute,* the innocent receiving the penalty we deserved. "The wages of sin is death" (Romans 6:23) Paul asserted. He also called

our condition "helpless" (5:6)—spiritually bank-
rupt. But Jesus paid those wages for us on the cross.

The word "substitute" means "a person serving
in place of another." Let's broaden the scope of
Bible passages that convey the concept of Jesus
serving as your substitute.

 Inspect Isaiah 53:4-7, Second Corinthians 5:21,
Galatians 3:13 and First Thessalonians 5:9-10.
Locate words/phrases from these verses that
convey the idea of a "substitutionary" death:

A _____

_____

_____

Pause a moment. Allow truth to permeate your
thinking. You may feel unloved, but the fact is "*Our*
griefs He Himself bore" (Isaiah 53:4, emphasis
added). He died "for *our* transgressions . . . for *our*
iniquities . . . for *our* well-being" (Isaiah 53:5, emphasis added). Jesus became "sin on *our* behalf" (2
Corinthians 5:21, emphasis added). He rescued us
form sin's penalty "having become a curse *for us*"
(Galatians 3:13, emphasis added). Why did He die?
"*For us*" (1 Thessalonians 5:10, emphasis added).

Maybe your self-esteem has been so severely tar-
nished by another's rejection that you still feel unloved. Initially, reading those Bible verses doesn't
seem to affect you. What you nod in agreement
with cognitively concerning Christ's death for you
still doesn't register emotionally. If that's the case,
keep reminding yourself of this maxim: *God's Word*

is more reliable than your feelings. And God's Word says you're loved, as demonstrated by Christ substituting for you on the cross.

Perhaps a graphic description of crucifixion will convince you of God's love. As you read the following explanation of this means of execution, remember that Jesus experienced it all *for you.*

In ancient times, a person was executed by crucifixion in one of two ways. The first manner involved staking or tying the victim to two beams of wood already joined to form a cross. Then the executioners hoisted the cross with the body, plunging it into a crevice already prepared in the earth or in soft stone. The second procedure required the victim to be staked or tied to a horizontal beam. Then the victim and horizontal beam were lifted and dropped into a slot of a larger vertical beam already secured in the earth. Most likely, Jesus experienced the second procedure.

Jesus' executioners drove nails through His limbs in order to fasten Him to the wood—far more excruciating than if He had been tied. When soldiers dropped Jesus' cross into place, the force probably ripped His shoulders out of their sockets. The shoulder dislocation meant He couldn't pull up the weight of His body in order to relieve pressure on His lungs. To avoid immediate suffocation, He pushed His torso up a bit by straightening His legs, permitting labored breathing. Yet any attempt to shift His legs exacerbated the pain caused by the spike in His feet. The breathing position lasted only a few seconds, then He would collapse and began gasping for air again. Jesus' body was racked by convulsions and extreme changes in temperature caused by the malfunctioning of His nervous system.

Yet even more agonizing than physical torture was the acute awareness of His Heavenly Father's abandonment. For the first time in eternity, Jesus felt alienated from God the Father. We cannot comprehend the extent of emotional trauma He endured, for there's no correlation in human relationships to the intimacy enjoyed by members of the Trinity. Yet, for a moment in time, God could not look upon His Son. He distanced Himself from His Son because Christ was bearing our sin, serving as our substitute. That explains Jesus' heartfelt cry from the cross: "My God, My God, Why hast Thou forsaken Me?"

You already know the answer to Jesus' question. Why did God the Father desert His Son? So you would never know the feeling of desertion. Why did He turn His back on Christ? So He wouldn't have to turn His back on you. That's love—with a capital "L"!

So What?

Knowing God loves you enables you to extend love to others. What you've experienced, you can give. Knowing you're loved boosts self-esteem. Who can doubt the intrinsic value of a person for whom Christ substituted Himself? Knowing God loves you, no matter what, releases you from bond-

age to other people. You no longer need to compro-
mise your convictions in order to obtain their acceptance. Their affection still matters to you. You're
a human being, not a feeling-deprived clone of Mr.
Spock (remember *Star Trek?*). Yet whenever your
ship is tossed around by circumstances, assurance of
God's love provides a safe harbor in which you can
drop anchor.

Want a case in point? Here's a heart-wrenching
story of how love releases God-given potential in
a person. The narrative tells how a Christian
teacher in a public school served as a conduit for
God's love.

> I know of a school teacher named Miss
> Thompson. Every year, when she met her new
> students, she would say, "Boys and girls, I love
> you all the same. I have no favorites." Of course,
> she wasn't being completely truthful. Teachers
> do have favorites and, what is worse, most teach-
> ers have students that they just don't like.
>
> Teddy Stallard was a boy that Miss Thomp-
> son just didn't like, and for good reason. He
> just didn't seem interested in school. There was
> a dead-pan, blank expression on his face and
> his eyes had a glassy, unfocused appearance.
> When she spoke to Teddy, he always answered
> in monosyllables. His clothes were musty and
> his hair was unkempt. He wasn't an attractive
> boy and he certainly wasn't likable.
>
> Whenever she marked Teddy's papers, she
> got a certain perverse pleasure out of putting
> X's next to the wrong answers and when she

put the F's at the top of the papers, she always did it with a flair. She should have known better; she had Teddy's records and she knew more about him than she wanted to admit. The records read:

1st Grade: Teddy shows promise with his work and attitude, but poor home situation.

2nd Grade: Teddy could do better. Mother is seriously ill. He receives little help at home.

3rd Grade: Teddy is a good boy, but too serious. He is a slow learner. His mother died this year.

4th Grade: Teddy is very slow, but well-behaved. His father shows no interest.

Christmas came and the boys and girls in Miss Thompson's class brought her Christmas presents. They piled their presents on her desk and crowded around to watch her open them. Among the presents there was one from Teddy Stallard. She was surprised that he had brought her a gift, but he had. Teddy's gift was wrapped in brown paper and was held together with Scotch tape. On the paper were written the simple words, "For Miss Thompson from Teddy." When she opened Teddy's present, out fell a gaudy rhinestone bracelet, with half the stones missing, and a bottle of cheap perfume.

The other boys and girls began to giggle and smirk over Teddy's gifts, but Miss Thompson at least had enough sense to silence them by immediately putting on the bracelet and putting some of the perfume on her wrist. Holding her wrist up for the other children to smell, she said,

"Doesn't it smell lovely?" And the children, taking their cue from the teacher, readily agreed with "oo's" and "ah's."

At the end of the day, when school was over and the other children had left, Teddy lingered behind. He slowly came over to her desk and said softly, "Miss Thompson . . . Miss Thompson, you smell just like my mother . . . and her bracelet looks real pretty on you too. I'm glad you liked my presents."

When Teddy left, Miss Thompson got down on her knees and asked God to forgive her.

The next day when the children came to school, they were welcomed by a new teacher. Miss Thompson had become a different person. She was no longer just a teacher; she had become an agent of God. She was now a person committed to loving her children and doing things for them that would live on after her. She helped all the children, but especially the slow ones, and especially Teddy Stallard. By the end of that school year, Teddy showed dramatic improvement. He had caught up with most of the students and was even ahead of some.

She didn't hear from Teddy for a long time. Then one day, she received a note that read:

Dear Miss Thompson:

I wanted you to be the first to know. I will be graduating second in my class.

Love,

Teddy Stallard

Four years later, another note came:

Dear Miss Thompson:

   They just told me I will be graduating first in my class. I wanted you to be the first to know. The university has not been easy, but I liked it.

Love,

Teddy Stallard

And, four years later:

Dear Miss Thompson:

   As of today, I am Theodore Stallard, M.D. How about that? I wanted you to be the first to know. I am getting married next month, the 27th to be exact. I want you to come and sit where my mother would sit if she were alive. You are the only family I have now. Dad died last year.

Love,

Teddy Stallard

   Miss Thompson went to that wedding and sat where Teddy's mother would have sat. She deserved to sit there; she had done something for Teddy that he could never forget.[2]

Miss Thompson illustrates how a person who's secure in God's love can love others unconditionally. Allow us to share another true story that shows the effect of God's unconditional love. You'll read about a young man who shared God's love with others—all because he knew he didn't "have to" witness in order to receive God's love.

A small group of us were addressing the members of a prominent social fraternity at UCLA. After the meeting, among several men who expressed their interest in knowing Jesus Christ was one young man who insisted he meet with someone in our group who would be available just as soon as possible.

Over coffee the following morning, he said, "I would give my eye teeth to have what you men have. But there's one thing holding me back."

"What's that?" my friend replied.

"Witnessing," he said.

"What do you mean?" we asked.

"I know good and well that if I give my heart to Christ, I'll have to start telling everyone I know how to get saved," he muttered.

"Where did you get that idea?"

"It's no idea. Some people I know who are Christians told me so. They said if you trust Christ, that's part of your responsibility, along with praying, reading the Bible, going to . . ."

"Just a minute," my friend interrupted. "God says He takes us as we are. It's strictly a matter of trusting Him. There are no price tags attached."

"Aw, come on," he objected. "You guys are out witnessing. What do you mean, you don't have to?"

"We're doing it because we *want* to. It's a tremendous thing to share the life of Christ with people, but that doesn't have a thing to do with becoming a Christian."

We went on to explain to him the greatness of God's love, and how at the cross, Jesus Christ so totally removed the barriers from him to God, that even if there were something he wanted to do to help deserve it, he couldn't.

"Are you telling me that I could accept Jesus Christ right now, and never do a thing in return, and He'd still accept me?" he inquired, almost puzzled.

We assured him that was so.

"Well, if you *promise* me that Christ will come into my life today, and that I'll never have to witness, I'll accept Him."

"We promise," came our reply.

We prayed together, and he invited Jesus Christ to become his Lord and Savior. We went on to explain to him that God had forgiven all sin—past, present, and future—everything he ever had or ever would do was placed upon Jesus Christ. We told him about his new life that would never end.

"This is the most fantastic thing I have ever heard," he responded. "I can't believe that I didn't have to do anything to get it."

He walked back over to the fraternity house. It was about 10:00 in the morning. He approached the first friend he saw and said, "I've got to tell you the most amazing thing I have ever heard. Today I realized that I could invite Jesus Christ to come into my life, and that I wouldn't have to witness or do anything, and He'd still come in. This is the greatest thing I have ever heard. Isn't that fantastic!" And by evening, he had spread the word around the entire fraternity. Because he didn't *have* to.[3]

God may or may not channel His love for you through someone like Miss Thompson. And your reason for witnessing may not be the fact that you don't *have to.* . . . Yet the fact remains: *You are totally loved!*

Memorizing Scripture

Hiding the words of Romans 5:8 in your heart will serve as a constant reminder of God's love for you.

What is a Christian? The question can be answered in many ways, but the richest answer I know is that a Christian is one who has God for his Father.[1]
—James I. Packer

CHAPTER
SEVEN

You Are Incredibly Secure

The cartoon in a Christian magazine pictured a huge auditorium. Only three or four of the hundreds of theater-style seats were occupied. A large banner was pinned to the wall behind the seating area. Perhaps the wording on the banner explained the sparse attendance:

ANNUAL CONVENTION
ADULT CHILDREN OF PERFECTLY
NORMAL PARENTS

A sense of humor is integral to a wholesome personality. Poking fun at ourselves alleviates pressure and keeps us from taking ourselves too seriously. Yet for a mushrooming number of people the idea of a dysfunctional family is far from a laughing matter.

Growing up in a broken home is increasingly the norm rather than the exception. More often than not, it's the father who leaves the scene, creating within kids what one psychologist calls a "hole inside." The absence of a dad—or even the presence of a father who fails to provide a stable, supportive environment—spawns fear and insecurity within kids.

According to the dictionary, insecurity means "to feel unsafe" or "to feel apprehensive about, or lack confidence in one's immediate environment." When someone you depend on for love and protection proves unreliable, you're vulnerable to insecurity. The escalating number of family breakups has resulted in a proliferation of unstable persons who are unsure of their personal identity.

But if you're a Christian, there's good news for you. No matter what kind of family you came from, no matter how you describe your earthly father, no matter how apprehensive you may feel because significant people have let you down, the fact is that *you are incredibly secure*. That's because you've been adopted by the only perfect Father who ever lived: God Himself.

Identity under Construction

You've discovered that God's opinion of you is far more important than others' opinions—even more crucial than how you see yourself. The only valid basis for developing a healthy self-concept is Scripture. God's truth, not the false values thriving in our culture, provides the necessary raw materials for constructing an accurate and a sturdy personal identity.

Who are you? In contrast to someone who feels excluded or left out, you're someone who has been

personally chosen by God for salvation. In God's
eyes, you aren't a failure whom He condemns. Instead, the truth of justification means He views you
as *officially holy*. Rather than feeling ashamed because of who you were prior to conversion, rejoice
because you're someone whom He has *supernaturally transformed*. The divine power that initially
opened your heart to the claims of Christ is still op-
erative, eradicating hopelessness concerning areas
of your life where change is yet needed.

Though you may feel rejected, God's Word is
more reliable than your feelings. The fact is that
you're *irrevocably accepted* by God. Reconciliation
means that hostility between you and God has been
replaced by peace. You're also a person who is *totally loved*, as demonstrated by Jesus' substitutionary death for you on the cross.

This chapter adds another brick to the construction project called your personal identity. Like the
previous spiritual blessings you've examined in this
book, the launching pad for this study is Ephesians
1:3-7. According to 1:5, "He predestined us to
adoption as sons through Jesus Christ to Himself."
To the benefits of election, justification, regeneration, reconciliation and substitution, add *adoption*.
Let's examine the meaning of this facet of our spiritual position and its implications for daily living.

Understanding Adoption

How important is the concept of adoption in
Scripture? According to one respected theolo-

gian, "Our understanding of Christianity cannot be better than our grasp of adoption."[2]

Back in the New Testament era, Roman law provided a way for a man to obtain an heir even if he were childless. The man could search for an adolescent male to carry on the family name, then formally adopt him as a son. Usually an older male child was selected, rather than an infant, so some idea of the proposed heir's character could be determined beforehand.

God also seeks heirs to carry on *His* family name—females as well as males whom He chooses for membership in His household—except He doesn't pick us because we're worthy to bear His name. He adopts us, despite our poor track record, with the idea of transforming us over time.

Absorb the details in the following Bible verses: John 1:12, First John 3:1, Galatians 4:4-6 and Romans 8:14-17.

Q What words/phrases from these references reveal your identity as a member of God's family?

A _____

_____

_____

Q According to Galatians 4:4-5, what happened to make God's adoption of you possible?

A _____

_____

According to First John 3:1, what motivated God to adopt you was_____
_____.

Q Look at John 1:12 again. **What words in this verse reveal your part in the process of adoption?**

A _____
_____
_____

Imagine: If you have ever "received" Christ or "believe[d] in His name" (John 1:12), then you're among the persons the Bible calls "children of God," "sons of God," "heirs of God" and "fellow heirs with Christ." Your adoption into God's family occurred simultaneously with your salvation. Jesus' death on the cross took care of your sins and reconciled you to God, paving the way for an intimate relationship. Love served as the impetus for God's adoption of you. Putting your faith in Christ was tantamount to saying that you want to carry on His family name.

To expand your understanding of adoption, let's explore its benefits and applications in terms of three marks of newness. God's adoption of you resulted in *new relationships, new rights* and *new responsibilities.*

New Relationships

The most obvious relationship that begins with adoption is with your heavenly Father. Your pre-

vious Scripture search solidified your identity as
His child and heir. Adoption goes hand in glove
with the benefit of reconciliation: You were
"transferred from a status of alienation and hostility to one of acceptance and favor."³

By distinguishing the concept of adoption from
justification, one author explains the relational element inherent in this truth:

> Justification is a forensic idea, conceived in
> terms of law, and viewing God as a *judge.* In
> justification, God declares of penitent believers
> that they are not, and never will be, liable to the
> death that their sins deserve, because Jesus
> Christ, their substitute and sacrifice, tasted
> death in their place on the cross. . . . But justifi-
> cation does not of itself imply any intimate or
> deep relationship with God the judge. . . . But
> adoption is a *family* idea, conceived in terms of
> *love,* and viewing God as *father.* . . . Closeness,
> affection, and generosity are at the heart of the
> relationship. To be right with God the judge is a
> great thing, but to be loved and cared for by
> God the father is a greater.⁴

Your relationship with God the Son also changes
with your adoption.

Q Read carefully Hebrews 2:9-13. **Since His crucifixion and resurrection, how has Jesus Christ
described the people for whom He died?**

A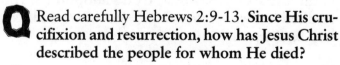

To label Jesus your "Savior" or your "Lord" is accurate. *But He's also your "Brother"!*

Adoption also changes relationships on a horizontal plane.

Q According to Galatians 6:10, what analogy did Paul employ to describe the people of God?

A _____

_____

_____

Q Read Romans 12:10. How did Paul describe the affection that should characterize relationships among believers?

A _____

_____

_____

Other Christians are your "brothers" and your "sisters." There's a sense in which you are a "blood relative" to every other child of God: What binds you together as a family is the blood of Christ! Your relationships with some "brothers and sisters" in the church may be far from ideal. Yet the fact is that God often ministers to you through the spiritual gifts and encouragement of others in His family.

Q Think of one "brother" or "sister" in the Lord whom you consider special. How does this family member facilitate your growth as a Christian?

Adoption gives you a new Father, transforms the nature of your relationship with Christ and dramatically enlarges your extended family. To these *new relationships* add a number of *new rights*.

New Rights

A "right" is another word for benefit or advantage. Your identity as an adopted child of God brings with it privileges and blessings. Your new rights include *God's protection*, *God's provision*, *God's palace* and *prayer*.

Protection

It's true that illnesses and accidents happen to God's children as well as to non-Christians. No matter what a person believes, physical death is inevitable. That's a carryover from the entrance of sin back in the Garden of Eden. Despite that reality, God often intervenes in the realm of time and space to protect His adopted children. He sometimes shields us from both physical and spiritual harm, either extending the length of our earthly life or warding off the enemy's attempts to derail us spiritually. We aren't always aware of His protective measures, but they're real just the same.

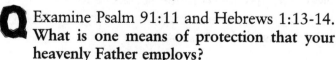

Examine Psalm 91:11 and Hebrews 1:13-14. **What is one means of protection that your heavenly Father employs?**

A _____

_____

_____

Q Now consult First Corinthians 10:13 and Romans 8:12-13. **How are you protected during bouts of temptation and spiritual warfare?**

A _____

_____

In Second Corinthians 10:3-4, Paul referred to "weapons of our warfare" that are "divinely powerful."

Q In addition to the indwelling presence of the Holy Spirit, what are some weapons God the Father has provided for your protection?

A _____

_____

Jesus Himself, your "Brother," employed one of those weapons on your behalf. He was interceding for future as well as first-century followers when He said, "I do not ask You to take them out of the world, *but to keep them from the evil one*" (John 17:15, emphasis added).

Provision

You could say that this entire book on *Discovering Your Identity* discloses spiritual and emotional provision of your Father. You've already discovered that He has filled your need for hope, acceptance, love and security. The spiritual blessings in Ephesians 1:3-7 are yours—lock, stock and barrel! It's all part of the inheritance you receive from your wealthy heavenly Father (Ephesians 1:11). He saved and adopted you because He is "*rich* in mercy" (2:4, emphasis added). His provision is sustained by "the surpassing *riches* of His grace" (2:7, emphasis added). He allocates to you "the *riches* of His glory" (3:16, emphasis added). A preacher's privilege is to convey "the unfathomable *riches* of Christ" (3:8, emphasis added). Your heavenly Father is "abounding in *riches* for all who call on Him" (Romans 10:12, emphasis added).

Yet His provision is more tangible at times too.

Q **What type of provision did the Lord promise in Matthew 6:25-32 and Philippians 4:15-19?**

A _____

_____

_____

Q **Describe a time when God intervened in your life to provide for you physically or materially.**

A _____

_____

_____

You've yet to receive part of your inheritance as a child of God. Let's look at another "right" Jesus' death earned for you.

Palace

Another title belonging to God the Father is "King" (Psalm 10:16). The Bible calls His management of the universe a "reign" or "rule." Where do rulers reside? Not in a cozy apartment or a run-of-the-mill house. Kings live in palaces! Eventually, so do His heirs.

Q Soak up the promise in John 14:1-3. **Restate the truth of these verses in your own words:**

A _____

_____

_____

Q What words in these verses reveal the emphatic nature of Jesus' promise?

A _____

_____

Did the magnitude of this ultimate benefit as God's child sink in? Your Savior and Brother, Jesus Christ, is continuing His earthly role as carpenter. He's preparing a place in heaven—the Father's palace—*for you*! Paul understood this inherited asset as indicated by First Corinthians 15, a chapter that teems with teaching on the resurrection. That's why he wrote, "O death, where is your victory? O death, where is your sting?" (15:55). The certainty of heaven, a future aspect of our inheritance, prompted one theologian to say, "For a Christian, the best is always yet to be."[5]

Your new rights owing to adoption include your heavenly Father's protection, His provision and an eternal home in heaven. To this list of rights add one more privilege.

Prayer

Viewed in the context of your adoption, prayer is conversation with a caring Father. The nature of this relationship should spur you to approach the Lord whatever your reason for praying. When He taught about prayer, Jesus employed the father-child analogy in reference to God's willingness to answer (Luke 11:9-13).

Mark 14:36 summarizes Jesus' pressure-packed prayer in the Garden of Gethsemane, the evening of His arrest.

Q How did His awareness of His identity as "Son" sustain Jesus at the time?

A _____

_____

_____

Q Also delve into Jesus' model prayer, couched in Matthew 6:5-15. **Why did Jesus instruct us to begin our prayers with an acknowledgment of God as "Our Father"?**

A _____

_____

_____

To start His heartfelt prayer, Jesus addressed God as "Abba!" (Mark 14:36). Now that you're adopted, you're permitted to use the same term (Romans 8:15). Back in Jesus' day, Jewish children used "Abba" when addressing their dads. The word connotes warmth and familiarity. Pious Jews never used "Abba" to address God, figuring it would be disrespectful and too casual. Jesus' example changed all that. His own intimacy with God the Father is now part of your inheritance since you're one of the "fellow heirs with Christ" (8:17). Knowing that God has the traits of an ideal dad should promote childlike faith and serve as an impetus for you to enter His presence.

With new rights, however, come particular responsibilities of membership in God's family.

New Responsibilities

Because of their lofty destiny, children of royalty are expected to behave in a way that enhances their father's reputation. What they say and do influence others' perceptions of the family name. They may even receive extra training and discipline to fit them for their high calling. Similarly, as a child of the King, your family identity should shape your conduct.

 Read First Peter 1:13-17. **Jot down words/ phrases from this passage that represent motivations for holy living.**

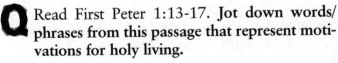

The text offers at least three valid motivations for obedience: (1) *a love response to God's grace in your life,* implied by Peter's reference to grace brought at Jesus' revelation (1:13); (2) *a desire to be like your heavenly Father, to reflect His likeness* (1:15-16); and (3) *the fact that all believers will eventually receive judgment—for the purpose of rewards, not regarding their eternal destiny—for their deeds* (1:17).

So your primary impetus for holiness is a desire to please and emulate a caring heavenly Father, not a sense of duty or compulsion.

 Also examine Matthew 5:13-16 and 5:43-48. How did Jesus' words reinforce a positive, rather than a negative, motivation for obedience?

A _____

_____

 In what one way is the Holy Spirit nudging you to act more like your heavenly Father?

A _____

_____

Adoption suggests that God's children should be distinguishable from other people. But sometimes that's not the case.

Q According to Hebrews 12:5-11, what action does a loving father take to expedite his children's progress toward maturity?

A _____

_____

Q As suggested by these verses, in what sense is divine discipline a privilege, or benefit, of adoption?

A _____

_____

Q How have you personally profited from what you considered your heavenly Father's discipline?

A _____

_____

You've discovered that adoption results in *new relationships* with God the Father, Jesus Christ and your siblings within His "forever family." You enjoy *new rights*, such as protection, provision, a residence in God's palace and prayer. *New responsibilities* also stem from adoption. You're expected to bear your heavenly Father's likeness. That responsibility isn't burdensome though, because you're proud to call Him "Father." You obey Him because you love Him. That's the least you can do in light of all He has done for you. As a result of His adoption of you, you're *incredibly secure*. God is one father who'll never desert His family members.

Memorizing Scripture

Learning John 1:12 by heart will serve as a perpetual reminder of your identity as God's child.

God is a much better judge of value than people who go around switching price tags.

CHAPTER EIGHT

You Are Obviously Valuable

Author Tony Campolo tells a story about October 31, a day of the year kids used to set aside for mischievous deeds. Kids all over a particular town conjured up creative ways to trick or terrify others on that particular date. One year, two boys came up with the most novel scheme yet. They decided to sneak into a department store after hours—not to steal items, but to switch the price tags. They'd take the tags off expensive items and put them on less expensive products and vice versa. The next shopping day, customers would find hairpins costing $20 and spot a 50¢ sticker on nice clothes.[1]

That's what some of us do on a daily basis. We switch the price tags. We assign disproportionate value to people and things around us. We cheapen what's costly. We inflate the value of run-of-the-mill items. Want examples? We swoon over celebrities and neglect genuine heroes. We exalt a person's physical appearance while minimizing his character. We consider a woman's convenience a more precious commodity than the life forming within her.

We elevate style over substance. We pay more heed to other peoples' opinions than we do God's.

With this inverted sense of values, it's no wonder we're confused over what gives a person significance. It's no wonder so many folks see themselves as worthless and inferior. It's no wonder we believe the erroneous price tags that other people, and Satan himself, have pinned on us.

The purpose of this book is to help you clean up the mess made by purveyors of false standards. To rearrange incorrect price tags mistakenly put on God's people. To put things in proper perspective so you'll have a keen awareness of what's priceless and what isn't. To familiarize you with truths from God's Word that place a permanent, impossible-to-remove sticker on you that reads: *OBVIOUSLY VALUABLE.*

Despite our real objective value, feelings of worthlessness and insignificance are rampant. Here's what happens when we devalue ourselves as persons:

- We're prone to give away our kisses and virginity for the price of a pizza and a soda.

- We forfeit our future for immediate gratification.

- We become classic underachievers, light years removed from our potential.

- We treat other people cheaply, figuring they're no more valuable than we are.

- We're suspicious or leery of people who try to love or to compliment us. We assume they have an ulterior motive. (How can they esteem us in view of the low price tag we stick on ourselves?)

What price tag do you see on yourself? If you're typical, at least on occasion you question your value. It's hard to feel significant when an employer doesn't value your work. When you're sick and no one calls. When no one says thanks for your volunteer work at the church. When your kids turn their back on your advice. When you aren't as attractive, as successful or as smart as others in your social orbit.

But God's Word assaults feelings of worthlessness with objective truth. He makes a direct hit on inferiority with this fact: *You are obviously valuable because of the truth of redemption.*

Purchase Price

Serving as a reference for your identity in Christ is Ephesians 1:3-7. God has personally chosen you for salvation. He has justified you, accepting you on the basis of Christ's performance instead of your own. By supernaturally transforming you, He erased shame over your past and instilled hope for future change. Even when you feel alienated from God, the fact is you're welcome in His presence thanks to reconciliation. He demonstrated unconditional love for you by putting His Son, Jesus, on the cross as your substitute. He wanted you in His family so much that He formally adopted you, providing security that not even the best earthly father offers.

Now the book's spotlight is on another biblical term that puts the loftiest price tag in the appropriate place: *redemption*. Referring to Jesus Christ, Paul wrote, "In Him we have redemption through His blood" (Ephesians 1:7).

The verb "redeem" means "to buy back" or "to purchase for a price." If you're in desperate need of quick cash, you take your TV or heirloom to a pawnshop. The clerk gives you a set amount of money, keeping your item for collateral. If you want to regain ownership of the item, you *redeem* your pawn ticket. For an inflated price you buy back what was originally yours.

In the spiritual realm, men and women were originally God's creation and His possession. Then sin entered the picture, enslaving human beings to Satan. Redemption means God "bought us back" at a price only He could afford.

Q Meditate on First Peter 1:17-19. **What was the "purchase price" for your redemption?**

A _____

_____

_____

Q **According to First Corinthians 6:19-20, how does God's purchase of you affect your current status or position?**

That's right: *You're God's property*! And whatever (or whoever) God owns, He cherishes. Whoever heard of royalty paying an exorbitant price for junk? Bank on it! If the King of the universe decides on a purchase, it's precious instead of inferior. That's why no one else's neglect or mistreatment means you're worthless. God is a much better judge of value than people who go around switching price tags.

Liberation from Slavery

From what were you redeemed? One use of the term "redemption" in biblical times referred to the purchase of a slave. Occasionally, the highest bidder was someone who loved the person being auctioned. He'd pay the price, then set the slave free. This backdrop of redemption from slavery enhances your understanding of what Christ did for you. You were redeemed from sin's *tyranny*, sin's *treatment* and sin's *torment*.

Sin's Tyranny

Tyranny refers to harsh, oppressive treatment. Despite its initial allure, sin soon becomes a cruel taskmaster.

Q Read Romans 6:16-22. **What analogy did Paul use to describe someone without Christ?**

Whether slavery is physical or spiritual, it's tyrannical. A recent magazine article described a scenario in Haiti. A four-year-old-boy was separated from his parents when fire destroyed their humble residence. Now he's "owned" by a woman who works him up to fifteen hours a day. The boy begins at 6 a.m. by emptying the chamber pot. Then he builds a fire, totes water from the well and cooks breakfast. Chores continue throughout the day, and he gets little to eat himself. He doesn't receive pay, clean clothes or Christmas presents. Unlike his boss' own children, the boy doesn't attend school. Nightmares plague the little boy.[2] The real taskmaster in this anecdote isn't the woman who controls the boy—it's the sin that controls the woman! She's actually more of a "slave" to sin than the boy is a slave to her.

 What example can you give of sin's tendency to enslave people?

Sin's Treatment

Sin not only enslaves a person. It also destroys one's future, one's relationships and one's God-intended potential.

According to Romans 6:21-23, what is the ultimate outcome of choosing sin over Christ?

 _____

_____

_____

Leonardo da Vinci's most famous painting is *The Last Supper*. As he worked on it, he searched for a human model whose countenance he would paint to represent Christ. He needed a face that suggested serenity, dignity and righteousness. Leonardo selected a fellow named Petro Bandinelli.

The artist worked on his masterpiece for several years. As the project neared completion, he needed one last model to represent the face of Judas, Jesus' betrayer who eventually hung himself in remorse. He wanted a countenance that conveyed pain, sorrow and the destructiveness of wrong choices. He found the man he wanted, bedraggled and sitting in a gutter. Leonardo painted his Judas, capturing all the rough-looking lines in the model's face. When he finished, the poor man said, "I have sat for you before."

"You couldn't have," responded Leonardo. "I would have remembered you." But the model persisted. "Yes I did," he countered. "I posed for you when you painted the face of Christ. My name is Petro Bandinelli." He proceeded to tell Leonardo that his personal disintegration was the result of a pattern of sin in his life.

Q What evidence of sin's destructive treatment have you either experienced or observed?

A _____

_____

_____

Sin's Torment

The effect of slavery to sin isn't just external. Eventually, it afflicts emotions and attitudes as well. Sin's torment is revealed in a riveting news story originating from a city in Oregon. A young man and woman, frustrated over their inability to overcome a drug addiction, chose a public venue for ending their torment. They secured a long rope to the rail of a bridge. The other end of the rope was two loops formed by means of a slipknot. They put the nooses around their necks and jumped. Their bodies dangled from the bridge in broad daylight until removed by authorities.

To emotional trauma, add the ultimate torment resulting from sin.

Q Look up Galatians 3:13 and Second Thessalonians 1:6-9. **What is the final torment or consequence caused by enslavement to sin?**

A _____

_____

_____

Paul referred to hell as a place of *eternal* destruction and separation from God. In contrast, the author of Hebrews described your redemption as *eternal* (9:12). Once God purchases you, Satan cannot ever buy you back! Imagine a sign hanging around your neck, written in the blood of Christ: *GOD'S PROPERTY—NOT FOR SALE.*

Responding to Your Redeemer

One implication of your redemption is the effect it should have on your self-image. That Jesus paid the price of His life for you should dispel forever feelings of worthlessness.

There's a custom on the remote island of Kimwatee. A man who wishes to marry must purchase his prospective bride from her father. Normally, payment is in the form of cows. A woman perceived as excellent or valuable nets six cows. For a good prospect, the father receives three or four cows. An inferior prospect garners only one or two cows.

Sorita was Sam Kuri's daughter. She saw herself as inferior and homely compared to other young women. As a result, she lacked self-confidence. As she shuffled through the village, she walked with shoulders hunched and eyes downcast. Sam figured he'd get no more than two cows for her.

One day, news spread that the richest man from a neighboring island was on Kimwatee looking for a bride. His name was Johnny Lingo, known as a wise and shrewd trader. To be selected by him would instantly elevate the status of any girl.

To everyone's surprise, after scouring the island, Johnny Lingo chose Sorita! "I want to redeem Sorita for my wife," he told Sam.

Sam secretly assumed that Johnny chose Sorita just to save money—or cows. He figured Johnny would offer only one cow, though Sam wanted two cows for her. He prepared for a tough round of bartering. When they sat down for the formal ceremony in which the purchase would occur, Sam opened negotiations with these words: "For my daughter, two cows."

What a shock it was when Johnny Lingo responded, "For your daughter, eight cows!"

As the years passed, Sorita's personality as well as her looks blossomed. Before long, folks considered her the most beautiful and regal woman on all the islands. What changed her? In her father's house she had been treated as a "one- or two-cow woman." But her husband perceived and treated her as an "eight-cow woman." Similarly, what God paid for you engenders a sense of intrinsic value and transforms your identity.

The fact that you now belong to God also has implications for your behavior. Just as your adoption results in a responsibility to reflect positively on the family name, (Chapter 7), redemption also serves as a catalyst for right living.

Q Consult First Peter 1:17-19, First Corinthians 6:18-20 and Romans 6:17-22 again. Add Titus 2:11-14 to the arsenal of verses. **Record**

words/phrases from these passages that suggest logical responses to your redemption.

A reasonable outcome of redemption is a fresh desire to please and to serve your new Master. This response to redemption has a parallel in the law of ancient Rome. Often a soldier captured during battle was released when a wealthy citizen paid a ransom. The soldier was then obligated to serve his redeemer until the purchase price had been repaid. There's a sense in which you are *forever* in God's debt and must surrender your life to Him, no strings attached. Except you can never repay such a purchase price, so you're in His service for good. *Paying off your debt to God, however, is not a loathsome or burdensome endeavor. To serve Someone whose Son died on the cross in your place is a privilege and a joy. Ironically, it is only in your bondage to Him that your true freedom lies.*

One passage you examined called for you "to deny ungodliness and worldly desires and to live sensibly, righteously and godly in the present age" (Titus 2:12).

 When you read that verse, what behavioral change is the Holy Spirit nudging you to make as a love response to redemption?

A

Remember a fundamental principle of marketing in the business world: *A product is worth whatever someone is willing to pay for it.* You were "bought with a price" (1 Corinthians 6:20). There isn't a price tag big enough to hold the number representing your value. That's because Calvary is priceless.

Memorizing Scripture

Whenever feelings of worthlessness surface, you'll combat them successfully by having memorized First Peter 1:18-19.

Guilt is such a screaming thing; forgiveness is so quiet. We often pay more attention to the noise of accusation than to the silence of sins forgiven. And guilt does not come from God. It originates from the lingering accusations of Satan. And we turn our attention to the accuser who condemns rather than the Christ who forgives. . . . What is God's analysis of the problem of stunted spiritual growth and development? . . . Our problem is that we've forgotten we're forgiven.[1]

—Peter Gillquist

CHAPTER NINE

You Are Notably Forgiven

A pastoral student at the school where we teach lost his left arm in an industrial accident. During a casual conversation, he explained a phenomenon called "phantom pain." Though years have elapsed since he lost the arm, David often feels the need to scratch the missing hand or forearm. Occasionally he feels a throbbing pain in the missing limb, as if the arm had just been crushed or bruised. Apparently, the intricate network of nerves centering in his brain remembers what it was like to have an arm and still emits "pain signals" as if the arm was threatened all over again. Because David's brain stores memories of past incidents that hurt the arm, painful feelings persist even though the physical limb no longer exists.

A similar phenomenon happens to many Christians. Their memory banks have a hard time forgetting past sins they've committed. They still feel the pain of self-reproach or guilt, even concerning sins they've confessed and abandoned. What they feel is an emotional type of phantom pain. They experience self-reproach despite the fact that, as far as God is concerned, the source of their pain no longer exists. The incident or mistake that created the guilt feelings is *not* in the portrait of them that God sees. Just as surely as David's left arm is gone, the wrong choice or moral lapse spawning the guilt is gone permanently from God's record books, removed by the blood of Jesus shed on the cross.

We can't resolve David's phantom pain, but we can prescribe strong medicine for the ache of guilt that may be lingering within you over past mistakes. It's a prescription that invades the mind, resulting in a different way of thinking about past sins. It's a truth that combats burdensome feelings with biblical facts. If Jesus Christ is your Savior, *you are notably forgiven*—no matter how you feel. According to Ephesians 1:7, "In Him we have . . . *the forgiveness of our trespasses*" (emphasis added.)

We know what you're thinking. You already know, cognitively, that you're forgiven. But do you grasp the practical implications of this truth? Has this particular "spiritual blessing" (Ephesians 1:3) seeped into your consciousness and affected the way you perceive yourself? Have you appropriated the fact that you're forgiven? Not if guilt feelings still haunt you. Not if you keep thinking that you don't measure up, spiritually speaking. Not if the weight of past sins still loads you down, resulting in self-recrimination. The purpose of this chapter is to disclose for you the significance of your forgiven state. Such a disclosure requires familiarity with a biblical truth called "propitiation."

Ready for your first dose of medicine? You'll find the taste sweet instead of bitter.

Defining Propitiation

Propitiation may be an unfamiliar term to you, yet it is integral to your identity in Christ and to relieving the discomfort of guilt. The word carries the idea of *satisfaction*. Put simply, "propitiation means that Christ satisfied the holiness of God so that He is able to extend grace and mercy to lost sinners."[2]

 Read Romans 3:23-26, then zero in on verse 25. **By implication, to what historical incident did Paul link propitiation?**

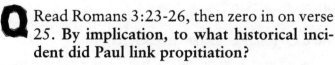

What the Bible calls "propitiation" is part of the gift package you received at salvation. The package came in the shape of a cross where Jesus paid the penalty for your sins. Jesus was the One "whom God displayed publicly as a *propitiation* in His blood through faith" (Romans 3:25, emphasis added).

You dissected the implications of Jesus' crucifixion in previous chapters. By putting your faith in Jesus' work on the cross, you were *justified* in the sight of God (Chapter 3). His righteousness was immediately credited to you. Thanks to His death, you were *reconciled* to God (Chapter 5). There's no more hostility or conflict separating you from Him. The fact that He died as a *substitute*, in your place, proves beyond a shadow of a doubt that you're loved (Chapter 6). He *redeemed* you on the cross, paying the exorbitant price of His life to reveal your value to Him (Chapter 8).

Now the spotlight shifts to one additional benefit of Calvary. *You are notably forgiven because of the effect Jesus' death had on God the Father.* Though propitiation benefits you, it has more of a "God-ward focus" than other spiritual blessings covered in this book. The following section explains what we mean by a "God-ward focus."

An Offense against God

Imagine that your daughter dresses elegantly for a banquet. Her date arrives in a sports utility vehicle caked with mud. Instead of ringing the doorbell and escorting her to the car, he honks the horn for her. Instead of dressing in a tuxedo with shiny black shoes, he's wearing faded jeans, a T-shirt and worn-out sneakers. How would you react to such a scenario? Anyone with one iota of class or character would feel offended. Miffed. Angry. That's the effect that somebody else's repugnant behavior has on you.

The truth of propitiation implies that our sin is an insult to God—an offense against His character. Our finite minds cannot fathom the extent of His holiness nor the purity of His character. How your daughter's date behaved doesn't have a fraction of the effect on you that our sins exert on a righteous God.

Examine the following verses: Romans 3:5; Ephesians 2:3; 5:3-6 and Colossians 3:5-6.

Q What words/phrases from these verses reveal God's reaction to sin?

A _____

_____

_____

Q How do you react to the idea of an "angry" God? Why?

A _____

_____

_____

Some people believe that assigning anger to God is inappropriate. They perceive Him as loving and not capable of wrath or a judgmental spirit. But such a view reveals a shallow understanding of

God's nature. To react nonchalantly to mankind's repulsive behavior would constitute a denial of God's holiness. His response to sin is *righteous anger*: "the *right* reaction of moral perfection in the Creator toward a moral perversity in the creature."[3]

If you *weren't* upset at the odious conduct of your daughter's date for the banquet, that would reflect negatively on your own character. Not to feel offended would reveal your own moral laxity. That's why a certain type of anger is consistent with God's perfection. One scholar's spin on God's wrath helps put the attribute in proper perspective:

> God's wrath in the Bible is never the capricious, self-indulgent, irritable, morally ignoble thing that human anger so often is. It is, instead, a right and necessary reaction to objective moral evil. God is only angry when anger is called for. Even among men, there is such a thing as *righteous* indignation, though it is . . . rarely found. But all God's indignation is righteous. Would a God who took as much pleasure in evil as He did in good be a good God? Would a God who did not react adversely to evil in His world be morally perfect? Surely not.[4]

Anger naturally expresses itself in action. Since sin is an offense against God, He must do something about it—or about the ones who sin. That leads us to the next element of "propitiation."

An Offering for Sin

God's anger in the Bible is an expression of His justice. The concept of justice implies that whoever commits an offense gets what he deserves: punishment. Look up Romans 6:23.

The prescribed penalty for sinning against a holy God is _____.

Being on death row, with all our appeals exhausted, paints a bleak picture. But here's where we have to factor in a different attribute of God. Consult Romans 5:8-9 and First John 4:9-10.

The attribute that compelled God to devise a creative payment plan for the problem of sin is

_____.

That's correct: God's *love* works in tandem with His justice to explain the concept of propitiation. God's justice demands punishment for sin. His wrath calls for decisive action against all offenders. *But His* **love** *for us stirred God Himself to satisfy, or to propitiate, His own demand for justice*! Jesus' death satisfied the prescribed penalty, leaving God's justice intact and revealing a depth of love that's otherwise foreign to human experience. Allow the following remarks to deepen your grasp of this truth:

> It was God Himself who took the initiative in quenching His own wrath.[5]

> The doctrine of propitiation is precisely this: that God loved the objects of His wrath so much that He gave His own Son to the end that He, by His blood, should make provision for the removal of this wrath. It was Christ's so to deal with the wrath that the loved would no longer be the objects of wrath.[6]

Jesus Christ satisfied the demands of the Law. Propitiation describes the *God-ward* work of Christ on the cross—He paid the penalty for the broken Law. The Law was satisfied. He bore the judgment of the guilty sinner, and sinners can now be justified. Forgiveness is now available. . . . There is no condemnation because Jesus Christ has died.[7]

For God to condone even one sin would defile His holiness like smearing a white satin wedding gown with black tar. . . . However, God is not only righteously indignant about sin, He is also a God of infinite love. In His holiness, God condemns sin. But in the most awesome example of love the world has ever seen, He ordained that His Son would die to pay for our sins. God sacrificed the sinless, perfect Savior to turn away, to propitiate, His great wrath. . . . While we were yet the enemies of God, Christ averted the wrath we deserved so that we might become the sons of God.[8]

Propitiation implies an offense against a righteous God and an offering for sin that enables us to avert God's wrath through faith in Christ. But there's yet another aspect to the truth of propitiation.

An Overthrow of Guilt

The chapter on reconciliation emphasized that the instant you put your faith in Christ, *God's favor was restored.* He's no longer angry at anyone who has received His Son as Savior. Lingering anger on God's part toward a Christian would mean that Jesus' death was insufficient payment—that God wasn't satisfied with Jesus' sacrifice. And that notion is too absurd to consider! To that truth add the primary implication of propitiation: *God's forgiveness is received.*

To rivet the fact of your forgiven state deeper into your consciousness, read Hebrews 10:17-18. (These verses were written in the context of a chapter explaining the sufficiency of Jesus' sacrifice for sin.)

Q **Summarize the truth of Hebrews 10:17-18 in your own words (fifteen words or less):**

 _____

_____

_____

Imagine: The blood of Jesus erases your sins from God's memory! And His forgetfulness regarding your sin suggests that He doesn't nag you about your past. Digest Romans 8:1. **What word does *not* describe God's attitude toward you as Christian? _____.**

God's forgetfulness about your sin and His lack of condemnation does *not* imply that He takes your wrongdoing lightly. He loves you just as you are, but He doesn't want you to stay that way. So when you sin as a Christian, the Holy Spirit convicts you in an effort to restore broken fellowship with God the Father. But don't confuse *conviction* with *guilt*.

Conviction is the Holy Spirit's way of revealing the error of our conduct in light of God's standard and truth. His motivation is love, protection and correction. Conviction should lead to confession—or an agreement that we've sinned against God (1 John 1:9). Conviction focuses on our behavior and helps us avert painful consequences of continued disobedience.[9]

In contrast, the Bible never refers to guilt as a feeling or a negative attitude toward oneself. Guilt refers exclusively to an objective state before God. A person is "guilty" before God only when he has not trusted in Christ's payment for his sins. A person may not *feel* guilty, yet *be* guilty in relation to God. Conversely, a person may *feel* guilty before God even though he has been declared "not guilty!" because of his faith in Christ.

Our contention is that a grasp of propitiation clarifies your forgiven status before God, and overthrows inappropriate guilt feelings that badger you. The discomfort of divine conviction is temporary and leads to positive change. The discomfort of guilt is ongoing and leads to an endless cycle of despair and self-reproach. Perhaps Peter was thinking of the paralyzing effect of guilt when he referred to Christians who had "forgotten [their] purification from . . . former sins" (2 Peter 1:9).

Seconds before He died on the cross, Jesus put an exclamation point to the truth of this chapter. He cried aloud, "It is finished!" (John 19:30). The phrase He uttered is the same one written on receipts during first-century business transactions. When the final installment of a loan was paid, the person receiving the payment would scribble on a document, "It is finished." The phrase literally means, "It has been paid in full!" The next time guilt feelings vie for your attention, meditate on a biblical fact. Jesus has "paid in full" for your sins!

What would you think of someone who made forty years of payments to satisfy a thirty-year mortgage? Foolish. Unnecessary. Wasteful. That's what we're doing when we mope around feeling guilty for debts Jesus assumed on the cross.

Memorizing Scripture

The launching pad for all aspects of your spiritual position that we've covered is Ephesians 1:3-7. This week, start the process of memorizing this entire passage. Study Ephesians 1:3-4 until you can recite it word-perfectly.

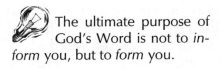 The ultimate purpose of God's Word is not to *inform* you, but to *form* you.

Living in Light of Who You Are

After David Bennett climbed Mount Everest, a reporter posed a question: "How did you do it?" The brutal cold and high winds make the ascent a dangerous, physically taxing endeavor. In his response, Bennett told how he protected himself from the assault of the weather, how he prepared his food and how he camped frequently in order to rest. Then the reporter who originally fired the question interrupted him. "No! That's not what I mean. I want to know how you climbed Mount Everest having only one leg!" Bennett's answer? "One hop at a time."[1]

When it comes to living in light of your position in Christ, you do it one step at a time. You dare to believe what Scripture says about you. You dare to make choices based on God's perception of you, not based on cultural values. Like ascending Mount Everest on just one leg, the task may seem impossible. But the next hop *is* manageable. Before you know it, you have reached the pinnacle of a new life.

Paul had the possibility of a transformed identity in mind when he wrote Romans 5:17. He was citing a contrast between the first man, Adam, and Jesus Christ: "For if by the transgression of the one, death reigned through the one, much more those who receive the abundance of grace and of the gift of righteousness will reign in life through the One, Jesus Christ."

The purpose of this chapter is to facilitate your application of the truths in Ephesians 1:3-7. You will reflect on your identity as described in Chapters 2-9 and receive direction for assuming that identity. Now that you know who you are in Christ, how can you appropriate that identity? The next few pages may provide just the boost you need to make it to the top.

Involve the Holy Spirit

A famous preacher once told his audience, "My job is to communicate God's truth. But I can only reach your ears. The Holy Spirit must shuttle the truth from your ears to your heart."

Bull's-eye! Before the truths concerning your spiritual identity can permeate your thinking and affect your emotions, you must involve the Holy Spirit through concentrated times of prayer. Overcoming feelings of failure, shame, rejection, insecurity or worthlessness isn't just a human endeavor. All the willpower in the world won't insure your application of the truths we've covered. Just as conversion requires divine activity resulting in a change of heart, maturing is also a process requiring divine enablement. It's the job of the Holy Spirit to remind you of your spiritual position in the warp and woof of daily living. It's the power of the Holy Spirit that can wean you from the false values of society and help you see yourself as God sees you.

Q Look up Romans 8:16-17. **What words in these verses indicate how the Holy Spirit convinces you of your identity?**

A _____

_____

Q According to these verses, **what aspects of your identity does He try to impress on you?**

A _____

_____

Q Now examine First Corinthians 2:9-16. **Why is involvement of the Holy Spirit essential to an understanding of your position in Christ?**

A _____

_____

Q Also read Ephesians 1:18-19. Paul relied on the Spirit of God to work in the lives of the Ephesians. **How did he express his dependence on the Holy Spirit?**

Whether the concern is your own growth or the needs of others, dependence on the Spirit's involvement is always expressed through prayer. Paul's goal for them was "that *the eyes of your heart* may be enlightened" (1:18, emphasis added). When you ask the Lord to remind you of who you are in Christ or to eradicate negative feelings that plague you, you are essentially asking for the same thing as Paul. The cry of your heart is, *"Lord, open my spiritual eyes!"*

If you're tired of the status quo in your life, remember the words of missionary spokesman David Bryant: *"Prayer is rebellion against the status quo!"*

Meditate on the Truth

In the opening chapter of this book, you identified false standards of worth prevalent in society: *appearance, achievement, aptitude* and *accumulations.* You also learned that the primary antidote to the effect of such erroneous thinking is a steady diet of truth. Focusing on what God's Word says regarding your identity is the only way to counter what the world says. That's why ongoing meditation on the truths covered in Chapters 1-9 is a prerequisite for your appropriation of these concepts.

Q Examine Romans 12:2. **According to this verse, how can a Christian wean himself from the false values that govern the world?**

A _____

_____

_____

The avenue of transformation is the mind. That's why we've encouraged Scripture memorization throughout this book. Hiding key verses in your heart that delineate your spiritual position provides fuel for the Holy Spirit to use whenever you're tempted by old ways of thinking and acting. Dallas Willard echoes our emphasis on Scripture memorization and meditation:

> As a pastor, teacher, and counselor, I have repeatedly seen the transformation of inner and outer life that comes simply from memorization and meditation upon Scripture. Personally, I would never undertake to pastor a church or guide a program of Christian education that did not involve a continuous program of memorization of the choicest passages of Scripture for people of all ages. . . .
>
> We *meditate* on what comes before us; that is, we withdraw into silence where we prayerfully and steadily focus upon it. In this way its meaning for us can emerge and form us as God works in the depths of our heart, mind, and soul. We devote long periods of time to this. Our prayer as we study meditatively is always that God would meet with us and speak specifically to us, for ultimately the Word of God is God speaking.[2]

Regarding your memory verses in this book, to what extent have you meditated on the truths they convey? Has your memorization been rote, or have you mulled over the implications of verses you've recited? Complete the sentence that follows:

The memory verse from this book that's left the greatest impression on me so far is _____ **because** _____.

Trust the Facts, Not Your Feelings

Remember a basic axiom for Christian living: *God's Word is more reliable than your feelings.* When you fail, you may feel that God no longer loves you. But Chapter 6 revealed that God's love for you is unconditional. If necessary, repeat the above axiom to yourself every time your feelings counter what Scripture says about you. It's a way to tell yourself the truth and combat the deception of Satan.

This strategy for assuming your identity in Christ emphasizes the role of faith. You involve the power of God's Spirit through prayer. You meditate on the truth concerning who you are. Now it's time to trust in those biblical facts concerning your identity.

Q Soak up the words of Hebrews 11:6. **Why is faith on the part of God's children so crucial?**

A _____

_____

_____

Discussing the role of faith in applying what you're learning necessarily involves a look at how *faith* relates to *facts* and *feelings*. Your spiritual position—including elements such as justification, reconciliation, and adoption—is rooted in historical *facts*. Jesus came to earth, died on the cross as the perfect substitute for sinful humanity, then rose from the dead. Who you are depends wholly on facts—what He did for you and what His Word says about you.

When you became a Christian, you exercised *faith* in the reliability of the facts concerning Jesus Christ. Now, as a believer, experiencing the benefits of your spiritual position also requires faith . . . faith in the facts of your identity as outlined in God's Word. Colossians 2:6 says, "Therefore as you have received Christ Jesus the Lord, so walk in Him." You received Christ by faith (Ephesians 2:8). Now faith is what enables you to experience or appropriate the facts of your position in Christ.

Whenever you put faith in the facts of Scripture, you may or may not experience positive *feelings*. Feelings are fickle by nature. Feelings fluctuate over time. Feelings aren't always rational. There may be no logical reason to feel a particular way, yet you do. So feelings aren't a worthy object of your faith. Yet you *can* bank on the trustworthiness of God's Word. Jesus Himself told God the Father, "Sanctify them in the truth; Your word is truth" (John 17:17).

Now, let's review. **Feelings aren't a solid basis for faith because** _____.
The most reliable basis for faith is _____
_____.

Imagine you had to arrange the three Fs in a logical sequence. **Which would you put**

First _____
Second _____
Third _____
Why? _____

Perhaps a diagram of an old steam-powered train can summarize the relationship among the three F's. Label each car with one of the three Fs. Which is best represented by the locomotive, essential to the train's movement? Which represents the coal car, the part of the train that provides fuel for the loco-motive? Which is symbolized by the caboose, tagging along at the end?

Choose to Live in Light of Truth

Previously, you read that assuming your identity in Christ requires the work of God's Spirit. Overcoming the plague of negative feelings associated with low self-esteem isn't merely a matter of human effort. *Yet the need to tap into God's power through prayer does not eliminate responsibility on your part.*

God has created you with the capacity to choose. When it comes to specific commands in His Word, you may choose to obey them or to disregard them. Similarly, you have the freedom to choose a new identity based on God's Word. Appropriating your position in Christ involves a mysterious blend of the Holy Spirit's work in you and your own decisions to accept the truths you've covered in this book.

Q The role of your choices is implied by numerous commands in the New Testament. For instance, set your scope on Ephesians 4:22-24. **What key phrases in these verses represent commands for believers?**

 A _____

_____

_____

"Lay aside the old self" (4:22) includes discarding the self-image shaped by the world's value system. "Be renewed in the spirit of your mind" (4:23) suggests the pivotal role of meditating on aspects of your position in Christ, as seen in Ephesians 1:3-7. Keep reminding yourself of who *God* says you are. "Put on the new self" (4:24) implies behaving and making choices on the basis of your identity in Christ. The imperative form of these

verses indicates that you aren't passive in the process of transformation. God expects you to take
daily steps in light of who you are in Christ, not
on the basis of how you feel.

Want examples of what we mean? Because you
know you are *notably forgiven*, you can "put on
the new self" by choosing not to dwell on a past
failure, but rejoice instead over the wisdom you
learned from your mistake. Knowing you are *justified* in God's sight and *irrevocably accepted* by
Him due to the truth of reconciliation, you can
"lay aside the old self" by choosing to remove the
overload from your schedule. You no longer need
to justify your worth by saying "yes" to every opportunity. Nor do you have to please everyone in
order to feel good about yourself.

Remember David Bennett, who climbed Mount
Everest on just one leg? He kept choosing to take
one more step—until he reached the peak. Similarly, you can choose a new path of life, knowing
that the resources of God's Spirit are at your disposal.

Express Your Gratitude to God

Because you're the object of God's grace, let
Him be the object of your gratitude. When you
thank Him for choosing you, justifying you,
transforming you, reconciling you, substituting
His Son on the cross for you, adopting you, redeeming you and forgiving you, the expression of
gratitude rivets those truths even deeper into your

consciousness. It's actually a form of review that expedites your experience of the truths. Here's how one author put it: "A thankful heart enjoys blessings twice: when they're received and when they're remembered."[3]

Besides, gratitude isn't optional for a Christian. It's a command: "Therefore, since we receive a kingdom which cannot be shaken, *let us show gratitude*, by which we may offer to God an acceptable service with reverence and awe" (Hebrews 12:28, emphasis added).

 To serve as a catalyst for your expression of gratitude, read Ephesians 2:1-7. **Jot down specific reasons cited by the text for being grateful to God.**

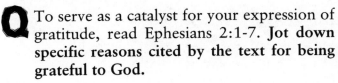

How can you assume your identity as a "child of the King?"

- Involve the Holy Spirit through prayer.

- Meditate on the truth concerning your position in Christ.

- Trust the facts concerning your identity— not your feelings.

- Choose to live in light of God's truth.

- Express your gratitude to God.

Memorizing Scripture

Review verses 3-4 of Ephesians 1, and add verses 5-6 to your memory bank.

When I talk with people, I don't call them laymen. A layman is a second-class citizen! I am a layman in regard to law because I haven't passed the bar exam; thus, I am not allowed to practice law. There is no such place in the Church of Jesus Christ for those who cannot practice. I say to people, "You are not a layman, you are a 'Minister of Common Life.' "[1]

—Elton Trueblood

CHAPTER ELEVEN

You Are Undeniably Useful

The pastor of a large midwestern church designed a questionnaire listing fourteen separate categories of traditional pastoral activity and responsibility (studying, counseling, visitation, committee meetings, teaching, etc.). He gave the questionnaire to twenty-eight lay officers in the church—members of boards and key committees. Each layperson was asked to indicate how many hours per week he thought the pastor should devote to each of the fourteen categories of responsibility. (Keep in mind that there are 168 total hours in a week. Also, the categories of pastoral activity did not include time for meals, for sleeping or leisure of any kind.)

By adding the number of hours in each of the fourteen categories, you come up with the total number of hours they expected the pastor to work each week. Here are the eye-popping results:

- 18 of the 28 questionnaires totaled more than 100 weekly hours of expected pastoral endeavor.

- 11 of the 28 respondents called for more than 140 hours per week.

- 8 of the 28—no kidding, folks!—expected involvement that totaled more than 168 hours per week!

- Overall, the average weekly expectation was 136.5 hours of pastoral activity per week.

These questionnaire results reveal the unrealistic expectations some church members have toward their pastoral staff. The data also suggests that there is widespread misunderstanding among believers concerning their spiritual identity. It's commonplace to perceive the professionals as the only "ministers" in the congregation. After all, they're the ones who are paid to do God's work! Yet the fact is that everyone who knows Jesus Christ is "called to ministry" not as a vocation but as a lifestyle; not as a way of earning a living but as a way of glorifying the One who saved them.

Your identity in Christ isn't complete until you comprehend your God-intended role as His ser-

vant on planet earth. Many who claim a relationship with Christ sense that their lives are
insignificant. They feel useless, as if their lives
aren't counting for anything that lasts. They feel
aimless, even bored, feverishly searching for
something that will give their lives meaning this
side of heaven. But that isn't the listless kind of
life that God intends for you. Grasp and apply the
truth of this chapter, and your life will be marked
by adventure instead of boredom, excitement instead of passivity, substance instead of emptiness
and direction instead of aimlessness.

Reviewing Your Position

From Ephesians 1:3-7, you've identified numerous spiritual benefits or aspects of your identity as a
Christian. God *personally chose you* for salvation.
You are officially holy in His sight, thanks to the
truth of justification. Because the Holy Spirit regenerated your heart, *you are supernaturally transformed.* Due to the truth of reconciliation, *you are
irrevocably accepted* by God. Because Jesus died in
your place on the cross, *you know you are totally
loved.* The moment you put your faith in Christ for
salvation, you became *incredibly secure*, owing to
God's adoption of you. Christ's death also resulted
in your redemption, suggesting that *you are obviously valuable.* And, as implied by the truth of propitiation, *you are notably forgiven.*

The final aspect of your identity in Christ isn't
couched in Ephesians 1:3-7. But you'll see be-

yond a shadow of a doubt that it's just as biblical as the other blessings that constitute your spiritual position. This final emphasis injects purpose and stimulation into an otherwise prosaic life. Because Scripture depicts you as a vital member of the Lord's task force, *you are undeniably useful.* Your usefulness to the Lord is also an outgrowth of your position as seen in Ephesians 1:3-7. The more secure you are in your spiritual identity, the greater your readiness for God to use you. Put simply, *doing* always flows out of *being.*

A Noble Identity

Ask folks in your church what comes to mind when they see or hear the word "minister," and you'll receive associations similar to the following: a church staff member, a clergyman's collar or TV evangelist, a seminary degree displayed in their pastor's office or a well-known musician whose life-sized poster greets them when they enter the local Christian bookstore. Yet as a follower of Christ, when you see or hear the term you should envision a snapshot of yourself. Integral to your identity as a believer is the mind-boggling fact that God has called *you* to serve Him!

Your identity as a worker for the Lord does *not* minimize the role of vocational church leaders. Though every Christian is given the privilege to minister in some fashion, not every believer is called or enabled by God to lead the church. The Bible calls for church members to respect and submit to their official leaders (Hebrews 13:7, 17). Their primary responsibility, though, is to prepare ordinary church members for a life of usefulness to the Lord (Ephesians 4:11-12).

Let's dig up the biblical roots of your noble identity as what one person called a "Minister of Common Life."

Q After investigating each of the following references, list words/phrases from the Bible text which show that every believer is expected to serve God, to help accomplish His work in the world.

A John 15:5, 8, 16 _____

_____

_____

A Matthew 5:13-16 _____

_____

_____

A Matthew 28:18-20 _____

_____

_____

A Second Corinthians 5:14-20 _____

_____

_____

A Ephesians 2:8-10 _____

_____

_____

A Ephesians 4:11-12 _____

_____

A First Peter 2:9-10 _____

_____

A First Peter 4:7-11 _____

_____

A First Peter 2:5; Revelation 1:6 _____

_____

Imagine: Whether you're a lawyer, a real estate agent, a housewife, a car salesman, an accountant or a university student, God wants to employ *you* to advance His kingdom! When this truth seeps into your consciousness, it ignites your passion and adds significance to everything in your daily routine.

Refer once again to the Bible verses you just completed. You hoisted numerous words/phrases from those verses that mandate every believer's involvement in God's work in the world.

Q What nouns from these passages represent specific titles or roles that God wants you to assume?

A _____

_____

Words that constitute titles or functions God has for you include "branches" that bear fruit (John 15:5); "salt" (Matthew 5:13); "light" (5:14-16); "ambassadors" (2 Corinthians 5:20); "stewards" of God's grace (1 Peter 4:10); and "priests" or "priesthood" (2:5, 9; Revelation 1:6).

Q Which of these designations impress you most? Why?

A _____

_____

_____

One designation that may surprise you is that of "priest." The New Testament clearly calls the Church, corporately speaking, a "holy" and "royal" priesthood (1 Peter 2:5, 9).

The primary implication of this designation is couched in a truth called "the priesthood of all believers." This truth declares that it is *not* necessary to approach Christ through a human priestly mediator. Instead, because of Jesus' death on the cross, every Christian has the privilege of direct access to Him without the necessity of a human priest as advocated by the Roman Catholic Church. We can approach God's throne confidently on our own (Hebrews 4:14-16; 10:19-22).

But a secondary application of our designation as "priests" is the opportunity we have to exercise a "priestly" function in the world—to serve as mediators who seek to bring sinful men and a holy God together. Both passages that mention this aspect of our identity include a mandate for ministry. After telling his readers that they were "A royal PRIEST-HOOD . . . A PEOPLE FOR God's OWN POSSESSION," Peter cited the ultimate purpose of their identity: "that you may proclaim the excellencies of Him who has called you out of darkness" (1 Peter 2:9). Similarly John asserted that through Jesus' death, we have been made "a kingdom and priests *to serve* his God and Father" (Revelation 1:6, NIV).

To sum up, our priestly privilege is to share the gospel so others will experience the same direct access to God that we enjoy.

Q How does the "call to minister" you've gleaned from Scripture make you feel? (Explain.)

Now, mull over the following remarks by well-known Christian authors. Allow their comments to improve your grip on this vital aspect of your identity in Christ:

> The Scripture declares, "According as each hath received a gift, minister it among yourselves as good stewards of the manifold Grace of God . . ." (1 Peter 4:10). From this passage it can be seen that every Christian has a ministry for which he is accountable to God. On this point there is no difference between clergy and laity. Thus when the layman is confronted with the opportunity to serve in the church, the

question for him is not whether he has a ministry, but whether this particular form of ministry is the one to which God is calling him and for which He will hold him accountable.[2]

— Norman Harper

The local church is essentially a training place to equip Christians to carry out their own ministries. Unfortunately, for many Christians the church is a place to go watch professionals perform and to pay the professionals to carry out the church program. In many quarters Christianity has deteriorated into professional "pulpitism" financed by lay spectators. The church hires a staff of ministers to do all the Christian service. This scheme is not only a violation of God's plan, but an absolute detriment to the growth of the church and the vitality of the members of the Body. Every member needs to find a significant place of service.[3]

— John MacArthur, Jr.

How ridiculous it would be if football coaches yanked their starting line-up off the field, and inserted themselves into the game to run the plays. Yet too often, that's what church leaders are doing! The leaders are the "star players" who pass, block and kick—while spectators watch and clap. But our job as leaders is to coach the church members so they can get into the game and succeed—while we clap and offer support from the sidelines. Like coaches, church leaders are successful when they've prepared others to get the job done.[4]

—Bruce Wilkinson

The declaration of Ephesians 4 is that the ultimate work of the church in the world is to be done by the saints—plain, ordinary Christians—and not by a professional clergy or a few select laymen. The four offices of apostle, prophet, evangelist, and pastor-teacher exist for but one function: that of equipping the common Christians to do the tasks which are assigned to them. Perhaps this can be made clearer if we diagram verses 11 and 12 in the following manner:

Apostles	**Do one thing:**	Unto: the work
Prophets	Equip the saints	of the ministry,
Evangelists		unto the upbuild-
Pastor-teachers		ing of the Body
		of Christ[5]

—Ray Stedman

Assuming Your Identity

How, when and where you engage in ministry for the Lord is between you and Him. Certainly, the needs in your own local church and community will provide a context for serving Him. Some ministries take the form of volunteer positions in a church: Sunday school teacher, committee chairperson, choir member, board member or small group facilitator.

Other avenues for service are more behind-the-scenes: personal evangelism among neighbors or work associates, befriending and mentoring a young housewife struggling with a fragile marriage, visiting people in prison or at a local nursing home,

praying regularly for your church staff and mission-
aries you know.

What you do for the Lord may or may not be in a
church-sponsored program. It may or may not be
public in nature. The scope of possible ministry outlets
is broad. God creates us with a wide variety of person-
alities, exposes us to a broad spectrum of experiences
and circumstances and enables us for service by dis-
tributing a diverse assortment of spiritual gifts. So *your*
ministries should be compatible with the particular
way in which God has put you together. He wants
your involvement in "kingdom business" to be a
source of joy and significance—not a burdensome obligation spawned by a sense of "ought."

What you've learned in Chapters 1-9 of this book
should impress on you the following perspective:
You do not serve the Lord as a means of earning His
favor or improving your standing with Him. You
cannot improve upon the favor and standing you already have as His child. Rather, you answer with a
resounding "Yes!" to ministry opportunities because that is who you are—a minister of God! You
also serve Him as a love response to a God who has
chosen you, justified you, regenerated you, reconciled you, substituted Himself for you, adopted you,
redeemed you and forgiven you. (Who *wouldn't*
want to serve that kind of God!)

Before leaving this chapter, evaluate your partici-
pation in ministry by pondering the following questions. If you aren't currently involved for the Lord,
allow these probes to jog your thinking about possible outlets. Tell God's Spirit you're available and

ask Him to reveal an opportunity that coincides with His plan for you.

- **What ministry opportunities exist within the programs sponsored by my local church? Which of these am I willing to try, at least for the short term?**

- **Who are some people (individuals or groups) within my community who have special needs, whom I can serve as an ambassador of Jesus Christ?**

- **What past experiences—personal as well as vocational—have prepared me for some form of service to God?**

- **What particular burden has the Lord given me for His work? (Has He put on my heart a particular age group within the church? A particular ethnic group or foreign country? A particular unchurched neighbor or relative?)**

- **What leadership or ministry training opportunities are offered by my church or by nearby parachurch organizations?**

What follows is a "Servant's Prayer." Read it slowly, then sign your name to it as a way of affirming and accepting your noble identity as a minster:

Father, my significance before You is based upon Christ's work on the cross. He paid a steep price for my sin. Nothing I do can make me more acceptable in Your sight. I'm a Christian because of what Christ has already done. Yet as an overflow

of who I am in Christ, and in loving response to
His work on my behalf, I accept Your call to work
for You in the various spheres of my influence.
You want others to know the Good News, and
Your plan is to accomplish the task through all
Your people, not an elite group of professionals. I
consider it a privilege to participate in Your grand
program on earth. Thank You for giving me the ti-
tle of "minister." I trust You to show me the par-
ticular forms my ministry should take, and to
strengthen me so my efforts will not be in vain. In
Jesus' name, Amen.[6]

Signature _____

Date   _____

Without a doubt, one of the most foundational
and significant ways to apply your identity as a minister is to share your faith with non-Christians in
your sphere of influence. Chapter 12 helps equip
you for this priestly role by explaining a "one-verse"
method for personal evangelism. May the next
chapter help you fulfill your identity as a *branch,*
salt, light, ambassador, steward and *priest.*

Memorizing Scripture

Continue your work in Ephesians 1:3-7. This
week focus on 1:7, plus review verses 3-6. Your current and future ministries should be viewed as a love
response to the benefits couched in this passage.

We have conditioned our-
selves into thinking that all
that really matters is that we should
be good, honest, clean-living,
churchgoing Christians. Now with
all due respect, that's a cop-out.
There are going to be souls in hell
who are convinced you were a
good, clean-living, churchgoing
Christian, and they'll be in hell because they never heard that the
gospel is relevant to them. Evangelism is not the added extra for those
who are that way inclined. The
church is in the world's debt. I'm
alarmed by the philosophy that the
sole task of the church is to turn out
nice Christian people. I believe the
sole task of the church is to turn out
people who honestly believe they
have the only message of hope and
that they are the only people who
have it.[1]

— Stuart Briscoe

CHAPTER TWELVE

You Are Christ's Witness

Look up the word "witness" in a dictionary. You'll see that the term refers to
someone who testifies concerning a fact
or experience, or one who observes a phe-

nomenon, then presents evidence of its reality. Study the term's history and you discover that "witness" stems from a word meaning, "one who knows." The only prerequisite for serving as a credible witness in court is firsthand experience or knowledge of the case under investigation.

That's why *you* qualify as Jesus Christ's witness in your sphere of influence! Because you've experienced a life-changing encounter with Christ, you're convinced that Christianity is *fact* rather than fiction. You've observed His work in your life since conversion. Your knowledge of Him is intimate rather than theoretical. What Jesus said to His followers right before He ascended into heaven applies to you now: "You shall be My witnesses" (Acts 1:8).

In Chapter 11 you discovered that *you are incredibly useful* to the Lord. Though not every Christian is called or gifted to lead, every believer *is* given the high privilege of ministering in the church and in the world. Biblical designations that imply a ministering function, and apply to all Christians include *ambassador, steward* and *priest*. Your identity in Christ includes your membership on His task force, your role as His servant. This aspect of your identity should eradicate the sense of aimlessness and boredom that characterizes so many of God's children.

Personal evangelism is one basic way to assume your noble identity as a minister for the Lord. View your role as Christ's witness as a natural overflow of who you are, as well as a love response to what He has done for you, not as some burdensome obligation that a Christian "ought" to fulfill. Remember . . .

- He has personally chosen you.

- He has justified you, declaring you officially holy in His sight.

- He has supernaturally transformed you, through what Scripture calls your regeneration.

- He reconciled you to Himself, removing all hostility that previously marked your relationship with God.

- He proved His love for you by substituting Himself for you on the cross.

- The instant you put your faith in Christ you were formally adopted into God's family.

- He redeemed you by paying the exorbitant price of His life on the cross.

- He has forgiven you, freeing you from an endless cycle of self-reproach and guilt feelings.

To witness for that kind of Savior is a lofty privilege!

A Strategy for Fulfilling Your Role

Assuming your identity as a witness requires an awareness of key Bible truths, plus a practical method for communicating these truths. What follows is a resource that gives you both the content and a workable procedure for effective personal evangelism. You'll learn to employ one Bible verse—John 3:16—to share the plan of salvation with others. Read the step-by-step explanation and accompanying diagrams carefully.

One Verse Method—John 3:16
Introduction

TRANSITION: Say that John 3:16 is the most famous verse in the entire Bible and that you want to show this person why.

ACTION: Take out a piece of paper and write the words of John 3:16 at the very top of the page in this particular order, leaving room on the page for subsequent steps. (To help you remember this order, note that the middle two phrases both start with the word "that" and both end with a reference to Jesus Christ.) Number these phrases in the following order: 1, 3, 4, 2. (See Step 1.)

John 3:16

1. For "God" so "loved" the "world,"
3. that He gave His only begotten Son,
4. that whoever believes in Him
2. should not perish, but have eternal life.

Step 1: Introduction

EXPLANATION: The reason John 3:16 is so famous is because it summarizes the Bible in four spiritual truths. If you understand these four spiritual truths, you will understand what the entire Bible is all about.

GOD'S PURPOSE

TRANSITION: Let's look at the first truth.

ACTION: Put quotation marks around the words "God," "love," and "world." Then, about halfway down the page, diagram this truth by writing the word "God" on the right, the word "world" on the left, and the word "love" down the middle. (See Step 2.)

John 3:16

1. For "God" so "loved" the "world,"
3. that He gave His only begotten Son,
4. that whoever believes in Him
2. should not perish, but have eternal life.

WORLD   L   GOD
                         O
                         V
                         E

Step 2: God's Purpose

EXPLANATION: God created man to have a personal relationship with Him. He wants this relationship to be one of love, one where God shows His love to people and where people show their love to Him.

TRANSITION: Why do you think that more people are not experiencing this loving personal relationship?

ACTION: Write the word "sin" below the word "love." Then draw two cliffs, one under the word "world," and the other under the word "God." (See Step 3.)

John 3:16

1. For "God" so "loved" the "world,"
3. that He gave His only begotten Son,
4. that whoever believes in Him
2. should not perish, but have eternal life.

WORLD   L   GOD
                         O
                         V
                         E

                         SIN

Step 3

EXPLANATION: It is because of sin. Sin is disobeying God. When someone is offended it causes problems in the relationship. Sin causes a separation between God and man.

MAN'S PROBLEM

TRANSITION: Let's look at the second spiritual truth. It says, "should not perish, but have eternal life."

ACTION: Put quotation marks around the word "perish" and write it under the left-hand cliff, the one with the word "world" on it. Then draw an arrow downward from the word "perish" and write the word "hell." (See Step 4.)

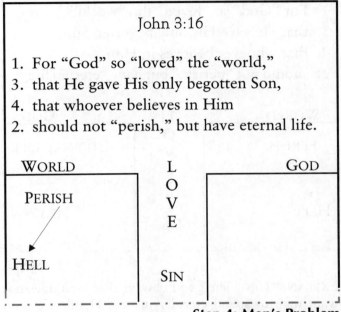

John 3:16

1. For "God" so "loved" the "world,"
3. that He gave His only begotten Son,
4. that whoever believes in Him
2. should not "perish," but have eternal life.

WORLD   L   GOD
                         O
      PERISH   V
                         E

HELL   SIN

Step 4: Man's Problem

EXPLANATION: It is bad enough to be separated from God and His love, but it gets worse. The Bible says that if anyone dies physically while spiritually separated from God, he will spend eternity in a place called hell.

TRANSITION: That's bad news, but this second spiritual truth also gives some good news.
ACTION: Put quotation marks around the words "eternal life" and write them under the right-hand

cliff. Draw an arrow downward and write the word
"heaven." (See Step 5.)

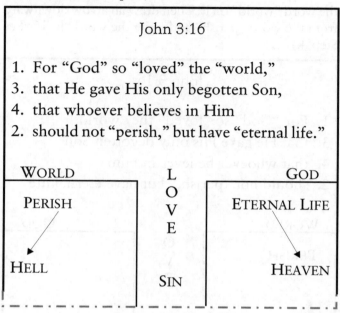

John 3:16

1. For "God" so "loved" the "world,"
3. that He gave His only begotten Son,
4. that whoever believes in Him
2. should not "perish," but have "eternal life."

WORLD   L   GOD
                         O
    PERISH   V   ETERNAL LIFE
                         E

HELL   HEAVEN
                        SIN

Step 5

EXPLANATION: The good news is that God does not
want man to spend eternity in hell. His desire is to
have a personal relationship with man so that they can
live together forever in a place called heaven.

GOD'S REMEDY

TRANSITION: The question then becomes: How does
one deal with his or her problem of sin? That leads us
to the third spiritual truth.

ACTION: Put quotation marks around the word "Son"
and write it on the diagram so that it shares the word

"love." Then draw a cross that encloses the words "Son" and "love" and bridge the two cliffs. (See Step 6.)

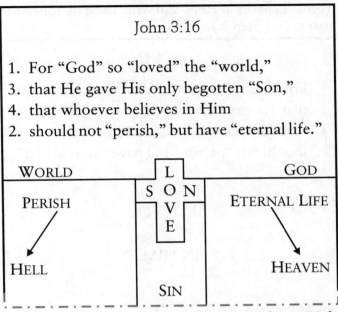

John 3:16

1. For "God" so "loved" the "world,"
3. that He gave His only begotten "Son,"
4. that whoever believes in Him
2. should not "perish," but have "eternal life."

WORLD — L O V E / SON / SIN — GOD
PERISH → HELL   ETERNAL LIFE → HEAVEN

Step 6: God's Remedy

EXPLANATION: God took care of the sin problem by sending His Son, Jesus Christ, to live a perfect life, then die on the cross in order that a person's sin could be forgiven. The amazing thing is after Jesus was dead and buried, He rose from the dead, proving God has the power to save people from a destiny of torment.

MAN'S RESPONSE

TRANSITION: The question now is, how can a person cross over the bridge that Christ has provided? The fourth spiritual truth gives the answer.

ACTION: Draw an arrow from the word "world" to the word "God." Put quotation marks around the words "believes in Him" and write them on top of the arrow. (See Step 7.)

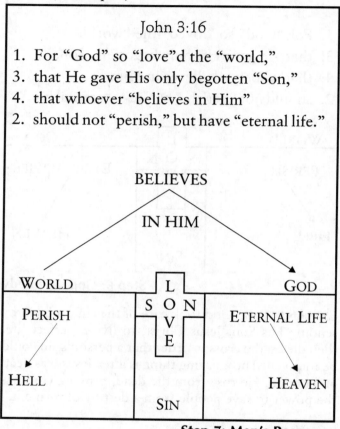

John 3:16

1. For "God" so "love"d the "world,"
3. that He gave His only begotten "Son,"
4. that whoever "believes in Him"
2. should not "perish," but have "eternal life."

BELIEVES

IN HIM

WORLD   GOD

	L	
	S O N	
PERISH	V	ETERNAL LIFE
	E	

HELL   HEAVEN

SIN

Step 7: Man's Response

EXPLANATION: It is not enough to simply know (1) that God loves you, (2) that your sin keeps you from that love and will ultimately send you to hell and (3)

that Jesus Christ's death on the cross spares you from
it all. It is only as you believe in Christ as your Lord
and Savior that you cross over the separation caused
by your sin and begin a personal relationship with
God. This word "believe" is more than just believing
in Abraham Lincoln. It means to commit everything
you know about yourself to everything you know
about Christ. It means to trust Christ and Him alone
to make you right with God.

INVITATION

TRANSITION: May we personalize this for a moment?
ACTION: Draw a circle around the word "whoever,"
then write the word "whoever" above the phrase "be-
lieves in Him." (See Step 8.)
EXPLANATION: The Bible says whoever believes in
Him will cross over to God and receive eternal life.
Where would you place yourself on this diagram?

- If they put themselves on the right-hand side,
  ask them to tell you about when and how
  they crossed over.

- If they put themselves on the left-hand side,
  or on top of the cross, ask the next question.

- Do you see anything keeping you from plac-
  ing your faith in Christ and crossing over to
  God right now?

- If they say "yes," ask them what their questions are and deal with them accordingly. If
  you do not know the answer to a question,
  tell them you will try to find out.

- If they say "no," prepare to lead them in prayer expressing their desire to God.

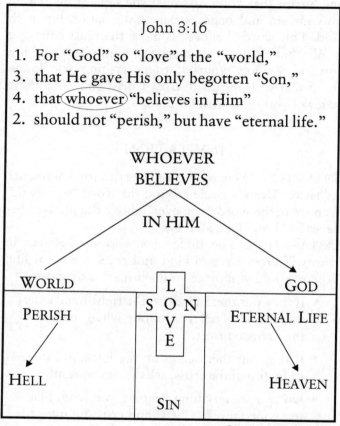

John 3:16

1. For "God" so "love"d the "world,"
3. that He gave His only begotten "Son,"
4. that whoever "believes in Him"
2. should not "perish," but have "eternal life."

WHOEVER
BELIEVES

IN HIM

WORLD   GOD

L
O
S   O   N
V
E

PERISH   ETERNAL LIFE

HELL   HEAVEN

SIN

Step 8: Invitation

PRAYER OF SALVATION

TRANSITION: If you desire to place your faith in Christ to make you right with God, it's as easy as 1, 2, 3, 4.

ACTION: Put the number 1 under the right-hand cliff, the number 2 under the left-hand cliff, the number 3 under the cross, and the number 4 beside the word "whoever." (See Step 9.)

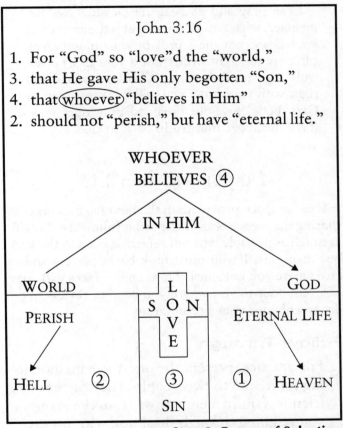

Step 9: Prayer of Salvation

EXPLANATION: If you would like to trust Christ you can do so right now. Tell God: 1) that you are grateful that He loves you, 2) that you are sorry for your sin that has separated you from His love, 3) that you are grateful that He gave His only Son to forgive your sin and 4) that you believe Christ will make you right with Him right now.

> I can pray and you can repeat after me. Remember, what is most important is the attitude of your heart, not the words of your mouth. You can pray the right words, but if your heart is not truly convinced that only Christ can make you right with God, then you will not cross over to God. Let's close our eyes and pray right now. (Pray the above four truths back to God.)

PRACTICING John 3:16

Use the space provided on the next page to practice sharing the message of Christ using John 3:16. Do this as much as possible without referring back to the various diagrams. If you must look back, place a smiley face where you got stuck. These smiley faces will serve as a reminder to you where you need to review in order to enhance your presentation.

Follow-Through

1. For practice, present the one-verse method using John 3:16 to two people. They can be close friends, family members or from the group, if you're going through this book with others.
2. Make notes of what you did best and on what needs more work.
3. Look for opportunities to build friendships or talk to non-Christians.

Memory Verse

To expedite your use of the one-verse method, memorize John 3:16.

APPENDIX A

DIGGING DEEPER

The Doctrine of Election or Predestination

This article isn't essential to your study in Chapter 2. Yet we provide it in case the references to predestination raise questions in your mind.

Covering Ephesians 1:3-7 is impossible without examining the controversial concept of "election," or "predestination." Paul wrote that God's personal choice of people for salvation occurred "before the foundation of the world" (1:4). God adopted us into His family because "He predestined us . . . according to the kind intention of His will" (1:5). Despite strong disagreement over meaning among Christians, the topic is unavoidable because Paul referred to it.

The Greek verb translated "chose" in Ephesians 1:4 means "to select" or "to elect." The idea is that humans have fallen into sin and cannot save themselves. God must act and, through a sovereign choice, determine who will receive His redeeming grace.

In its most elementary form, predestination means that a person's final destination—heaven or hell—is decided by God not only before we get there, but even before we are born! According to

one theologian, "God . . . chose some individuals
to be saved into everlasting blessedness in heaven
and others He chose to pass over, to allow them
to follow the consequences of their sins into eternal torment in hell."[1] The crux of the issue is this:
*On what basis does God choose some for salvation
and not others?*

Through the centuries, Christians have answered that question in two different ways. *One
common view is that God chooses on the basis of
His foreknowledge.* He selects for eternal life
those whom He knows in advance will choose
Him. This stance holds that God provides all people with enough grace to accept the offer of salvation, though not all choose to utilize that grace.
God predestines their place in heaven because He
is aware ahead of time who will choose to believe
of their own free will.

*A second position insists that God's choice of
some for salvation rests solely with God. He doesn't
elect anyone for salvation based on foreseen decisions that He anticipates they will make.* This view-
point says that left to himself, no fallen person
would ever choose God! A person's openness to
Christ depends entirely on God's initiative. The
faith a person puts in Christ is a divine gift. No one
chooses for Christ unless God has sovereignly chosen that person for salvation. "The elect do choose
Christ, but only because they were first chosen by
God."[2] God extends saving grace to some people,
but not to all. A common criticism of this stance is
that it seems unfair for God to save some and not

others. Proponents respond by saying, "The non-elect receive justice. The elect receive mercy. No one receives injustice. God is not obligated to be merciful to any or to all alike."[3]

This cursory look at election won't resolve all your curiosities or turn all your question marks into exclamation points. But don't miss the bottom-line implication for your life: If you're confident of a personal relationship with Christ, the *basis* for God's choice of you is a moot point! *The fact is He has personally chosen you.* This fact lays the first and widest plank in the platform called "your identity in Christ."

ENDNOTES

CHAPTER 1 - The Importance of Identity

1. Joseph Stowell, "Thinking Right in a World Gone Wrong," *Moody Monthly*, January, 1990, p. 4.

2. Adapted from Jack Canfield's "The Golden Buddha," in *Chicken Soup for the Soul*, Jack Canfield and Mark Hansen, eds. (Deerfield Beach, FL: Health Communications, Inc., 1993), pp. 69-71.

3. James Dobson, *Hide or Seek* (Old Tappan, NJ: Fleming H. Revell Co., 1974), p. 15.

4. As quoted by Steve Thurman, "Life, Liberty, and the Pursuit of Just a Little More," *Discipleship Journal*, Issue 53, 1989, p. 27.

5. Ibid.

CHAPTER 2 - You Are Personally Chosen

1. R.C. Sproul, *Essential Truths of the Christian Faith* (Carol Stream, IL: Tyndale House, 1992), p. xxi of "Introduction."

CHAPTER 3 - You Are Officially Holy

1. Charles Swindoll, *Growing Deep in the Christian Life* (Portland, OR: Multnomah Press, 1989), p. 238.

2. Sproul, p. 189.

3. Stuart Briscoe, from a transcription of a 1972 sermon on Romans 5 given at the Wheaton College Chapel.

4. Billy Graham, as quoted in Swindoll, p. 239.

CHAPTER 4 - You Are Supernaturally Transformed

1. Robert McGee, *The Search for Significance*, (Houston, TX: Rapha Publishing, 1987), p. 93.

2. Sproul, p. 171.

3. Ibid., p. 172.

4. Ibid.

CHAPTER 5 - You Are Irrevocably Accepted
    1. John Stott, *Men Made New* (Downers Grove, IL: InterVarsity press, 1966), p. 22.
    2. McGee, pp. 61-62.

CHAPTER 6 - You Are Totally Loved
    1. Charles Swindoll, *Growing Deep in the Christian Life,*. p. 240.
    2. Anthony Campolo, *Who Switched the Price Tags?* (Waco, TX: Word Books, 1986), pp. 69-72.
    3. Peter Gillquist, *Love Is Now* (Grand Rapids, MI: Zondervan, 1971), pp. 88-89.

CHAPTER 7 - You Are Incredibly Secure
    1. James I. Packer, *Knowing God* (Downers Grove, IL: InterVarsity Press, 1973), p. 181.
    2. Ibid., p. 182.
    3. Millard Erickson, *Christian Theology* (Grand Rapids, MI: Baker Book House, 1985), p. 961.
    4. Packer, p. 187.
    5. Ibid., p. 196.

CHAPTER 8 - You Are Obviously Valuable
    1. Campolo, pp. 13-14.
    2. Tom Hasland, "Slavery," *Newsweek*, May 14, 1992. pp. 30-39.

CHAPTER 9 - You Are Notably Forgiven
    1. Gillquist, pp. 23, 29.
    2. Warren Wiersbe, *Key Words of the Christian Life* (Wheaton, IL: Victor Books, 1982), p. 48.
    3. Packer, p. 166.
    4. Ibid., p. 136.
    5. Ibid., pp. 166-167.
    6. John Murray, as quoted in Packer, p. 167.

7. Wiersbe, p. 49.
8. McGee, pp. 78-79.
9. Ibid., p. 144.

CHAPTER 10 - Living in Light of Who You Are

1. Author Unknown, "Down and Out," *Newsweek*, August 17, 1992. pp. 46-47.
2. Dallas Willard, *The Spirit of the Disciplines: Understanding How God Changes Lives* (San Francisco, CA: Harper and Row Publishers, 1988), pp. 150, 177.
3. Croft M. Pentz, *The Complete Book of Zingers* (Chicago, IL: Tyndale House, 1990), p. 311.

CHAPTER 11 - You Are Undeniably Useful

1. Elton Trueblood, in *Leadership Journal*. Winter, 1983. p. 24.
2. Norman Harper, *Making Disciples* (Memphis, TN: Christian Studies Center, 1981), p. 121.
3. John MacArthur, Jr., *Body Dynamics* (Wheaton, IL: Victor Books, 1982), p. 94.
4. Bruce Wilkinson, part of talk presented to a church leadership class at Columbia Bible College, 1983.
5. Ray Stedman, *Body Life* (Ventura, CA: GL/Regal Books, 1972), pp. 80-81.
6. Terry Powell, *Learning to Serve* (Littleton, CO: Lay Action Ministry Program, 1989), p. 13.

CHAPTER 12 - You Are Christ's Witness

1. Stuart Briscoe, in a chapel message on evangelism presented to the student body of Wheaton College, April 1972.

APPENDIX B - Digging Deeper

1. Sproul, p. 161.
2. Ibid.
3. Ibid., p. 162.

MEMORY VERSES

Bill Jones is president of Crossover Communications International. Crossover is a missions organization helping to fulfill the Great Commission in Eurasia, currently focusing on the countries in the area of the Black Sea. Bill also serves as the program director for the Master of Arts in Missions and the Master of Arts in Leadership at Columbia International University in Columbia, South Carolina. A passionate communicator, Bill has trained thousands of people all around the world how to effectively share their faith in Christ.

CROSSOVER
COMMUNICATIONS
INTERNATIONAL

P.O. Box 211755   Columbia, SC 29221
Phone: 803-691-0688   Fax: 803-691-9355
www.crossoverusa.org

Write to Terry Powell or Bill Jones at:
CIU
P.O. Box 3122
Columbia, SC 29230
or call (803) 754-4100